INDUSTRY IN:SITE
101 TOP BEAUTY CAREERS

C. JEANINE FULTON

Copyright © 2008 by C. Jeanine Fulton

Published by Persona Market
1323 Gates Drive Suite A
Atlanta, GA 30316

P E R S O N A M A R K E T . C O M

Copyright © 2008 by C. Jeanine Fulton
Book design by Lance McBride
Cover design © 2008 Lance McBride

The Library of Congress Cataloging in Publication Data
Fulton, C. Jeanine
Industry in:site: top 100 beauty careers/C. Jeanine Fulton
p.   cm
ISBN – 13:978-0-9790027-0-0
1.   Personal care employment 2. Occupations 3. Job Descriptions

FOR GENERAL INFORMATION ABOUT OTHER PRODUCTS AND SERVICES,
PLEASE CONTACT **PERSONA MARKET** BY CALLING **1-888-504-8099**.

Printed in the United States of America

To my parents, for all that you do!

Special thanks to
Lance McBride, Elaine Penny, RoseAnn Perea,
Linda Long, Rev. Sue Hampton, Genia Church
and Cheryl Thomas
for your support.

FOREWORD

I knew that I wanted to be a beauty industry professional at an early age, somewhere between post toddler and puberty. Every Saturday morning I would set my doll's hair using hand lotion as setting lotion and pink sponge rollers for a tight curl. Then we'd watch cartoons while she sat under the pretend hair dryer, which was merely a lamp shade. It took about a week for the doll's hair to dry. On Friday nights her hair was styled with ribbons and bows, and on Saturday morning the routine began again.

As I grew older I became more fascinated with hair, make-up, and fashion. After high school I attended college and received a business degree in marketing. A few months after graduation, I enrolled in cosmetology school. Receiving my cosmetology license was by far one of the most exciting days that I can remember. The goal that I set years before while watching cartoons had been achieved.

Although I had received my license, it would be a while before I became a full time beauty industry professional. For years I worked full time in corporate America and part time as a stylist. I can remember day dreaming in my cubicle about finding a job that would allow me to have creative freedom. One day, after careful planning, job searching, falling asleep on the job and praying, I stepped out on faith. I decided to give 100% of my professional time and talent to the industry I love. Beauty.

Knowing the types of available careers is a key factor in having a successful beauty industry career. If you've picked up this book, you have a connection to this billion dollar industry. Maybe you are currently in cosmetology, esthetics, or barbering school. Perhaps you are a professional seeking new career options. You may be a high school student, college graduate, teacher, or dentist; the list goes on and on. The exciting news is no matter what level of experience you may or may not possess, this book will inspire you to explore the vast career options available in the industry.

As an educator, motivational speaker, consultant and now author, my life as a beauty industry professional is rewarding, fun and fulfilling. From hairstylist to salon consultant to beauty school director, to entrepreneur, each career move I have made has enlightened me on what it takes to be a real success in the world of beauty. Throughout the book you will see footprints. These are jobs that I have held throughout my career.

I'm sure that you too have goals and may have even gotten your start playing with dolls. After exploring careers in this book, your list of goals may expand. Remember, once a goal is reached, one must set another. My new goal is to empower industry gurus by sharing information, opportunities, and success stories. Discover your career path and decide how you can best use your talents to make your mark in this industry.

CONTENTS

CHAPTER 4 - The Salon and Spa Experience   119

AFTERWORD

ADDITIONAL TIPS

INTRODUCTION

YOUR CEO

" Knock, Knock!"

"Who's there?"

"Your CEO."

"My CEO?"

Yes, your **Character**, **Education** and **Opportunities**!

CHARACTER

Every job has specific duties and requirements. When recruiting, most employers and clients searching for service providers are looking for individuals with these professional attributes:

1. Excellent Communication – Exhibiting good listening and verbal skills, and using good writing skills when needed.

2. Team Player – Someone who can get along and work well with others.

3. Positive Attitude – The ability to leave drama out of the workplace.

4. Dependability – DWYSYWD! *Do What You Say You Will Do.* Be prepared.

5. *Teachability* – The desire to be open to learning new techniques, approaches, and systems.

6. *Great Customer Service* – The ability to make customers and clients smile and return for services and purchases.

EDUCATION

Many of the jobs require that one possess a professional license in cosmetology, massage therapy, esthetics, and/or barbering. Others may require experience or even a specific college degree. Each state governs the licensure of personal care workers. See the additional tips section in the back of the book for more information.

There were many jobs along my career path that I thought I should have been offered, but instead I received a rejection letter. Rather than singing the rejection blues for weeks, I decided to have a 5 minute pity party and then moved on.

While searching for the dream job I continued to develop my business, creative, cosmetology, and leadership skills. As Stephen Covey puts it, "Sharpen the Saw". The more education you receive and the more time and effort you put into learning your craft, the more marketable you will be.

Education can be obtained in a formal school setting, through an apprenticeship, on the job experience, and by reading magazines, books and other publications. Even if it means taking a class or two every year, the common denominator is "Learning."

OPPORTUNITIES

The United States Department of Labor, Bureau of Labor Statistics, predicts that we will see a significant growth in the number of "personal appearance workers" over the next few years. The statistics show an estimate of 14% growth from 2006 to 2016. Hair treatments for teens and baby boomers are expected to grow, and there is also the prediction of an increased number of nail and full-service day spas. Additionally the number of estheticians and make-up artists is expected to grow by more than 30%.

What does this all mean? I believe that the numbers say what industry professionals have been saying for years. People will always need beauty services and service providers. Our jobs, services and products expand far beyond those listed in labor statistics. There are careers in our industry that have yet to be created. Technology, time, and a new generation of beauty professionals will bring even more career opportunities.

For example, one day while I was speaking about the beauty

industry at a cosmetology school, a student shared with me her career goal. She said, " I want to have a salon on an airplane." "Hmmm, a make over jet," I thought. Why not? I encouraged her to stay focused, to keep dreaming and to develop a plan for her career. Who knows? With her CEO she might make it happen.

INDUSTRY IN:SITE
101 TOP BEAUTY CAREERS

SYMBOL KEY

The Make Up – Career definition and overview

Regimen – Daily job duties and responsibilities

Foundation – Job requirements including licenses, education and work experience

 Making the Cut – Advice on gaining a competitive edge

Highlights – Career benefits

@ **Tips** – Helpful websites

Beauty Marks – Success stories of extraordinary industry professionals

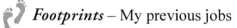 **Footprints** – My previous jobs

CHAPTER ONE
BEING THE BOSS

So you want to own a salon? We've found that the majority of students who enter into cosmetology school want to be salon owners. For two years, the Persona Market team of motivational speakers traveled to hundreds of schools across the US. Through Industry In:Site workmag (workbook/magazine) and motivational program for beauty students, we discussed career options with hundreds of future professionals. During each session we asked students to share their career goals, and salon ownership was always the number one answer!

The spirit of entrepreneurship runs deep within the veins of many beauty industry students and professionals. I'm also familiar with that nudge, urge, feeling, dream, heart beat, itch, drive, ambition and need to be a business owner. It is a paradigm that many share.

Owning a business in this industry is not exclusive to salons. There are many entrepreneurial avenues that one can take. Being the boss takes careful planning, education, hard work, determination, money and nerve. So roll up your smock sleeves and get moving!

"The only place where success comes before work is in the dictionary."
Vidal Sassoon

Shahin Ebadi Urias
Franchise Salon Owner
Sportclips
Tucson, Arizona

From Iran to Austria to Texas, the story of Shahin Ebadi Urias is one of determination and inspiration. In search of a better life, Shahin along with her then husband and first child left Iran. Their goal was to become US citizens, so they moved to Austria where there was a US embassy. To their surprise they became refugees in a place that was supposed to be their saving grace. The couple did not have work visas, therefore while in Austria they were forced to spend all of the money they had set aside for their move to the US. Fortunately after months of effort, the couple received green cards from the US embassy in Vienna with the help of a family friend living in the United States.

Initially Shahin and her family stayed with relatives in Texas. After saving five hundred dollars, the family moved out on their own into an empty apartment. "We spent $425.00 on the rent and used the remaining $75.00 for groceries." Not knowing at the time that they could have gotten assistance, the two began to "Work our butts off!"

While living in Iran, Shahin was the family hair stylist, cutting hair for relatives and family friends. Attending cosmetology school was something that she desperately wanted to do. Shahin decided to give it a try, however, when she went to enroll, school administrators advised her to take English classes. She could not speak or understand the language, nor could Shahin fill out an application for school.

For the next six months while working as a restaurant server, Shahin listened to customers and gained a better understanding of the English language. By this time Shahin had two children who were attending school and trying to learn English as well. "It was difficult for my children too."

One day while serving food, Shahin noticed the owners from the cosmetology school where she had applied. Although her English was broken, she told them that she was ready to try again. The kitchen manager where she worked volunteered to go to the school and help her fill out the necessary paperwork for enrollment.

" I worked and went to school full time. It was tough because I had two kids." In addition, Shahin had no transportation to school. She walked 3 ½ miles each way every single day. "There was no way I could get my 1500 hours to graduate if I didn't go every day." So, rain, sleet, or snow, Shahin arrived at school each day, and never missed. School was difficult because of the language barrier. Many times Shahin took her books home and translated one word at a time. After graduating, Shahin eventually landed a job in Texas with Sportclips, a salon chain with a sports theme. Because of her excellent service and skills, she was promoted to salon manager. "I turned the store around. It is amazing to see it become our third store in the nation." Now Shahin owns and operates her very own Sportclips salon. Her determination and dream of owning a salon is now a reality.

Amazingly, she financed her dream by saving "one dollar at a time." Her philosophy on money is to " Never spend more than you make. I became a single mom and lived on a budget. However, I owned my own house and car. My kids and I had a comfortable life. I put in many long hours at work, but I wanted to learn more and know more."

Independent, strong, and resilient best describe this beauty icon. She attributes these qualities to her childhood. At the age of ten, Shahin's mother passed away. "My brothers were younger than me, so I raised them." I learned to be tough and strong. Life goes on. I learned to move forward."

Shahin encourages her staff and others to "Be positive and to believe in yourself." What she likes most about her job? Being around people and putting a smile on their faces.

I. BEAUTY PRODUCT MANUFACTURER

The Make Up

Not many of us can live without beauty products. How many have you used today? Hairspray, lip gloss, facial moisturizer, shampoo, lotion, gel, and fragrance are all a part of our daily routine. Just about everybody uses some type of beauty product on a regular basis. Many well known brands used today were started by someone who saw needs and developed products to meet those needs. Through visionary effort, hard work and resilience they created a legacy.

Regimen

In the beginning much time and thought is put into the values, mission and vision of the brand. Creative ideas, development, and marketing strategies are then incorporated to begin the product's life cycle (the time and process from the development stage of a product to being purchased by customers). Product manufacturers work closely with cosmetic chemists to develop a product's features and benefits. They also work to secure distribution and retail avenues.

Foundation

Professional beauty industry experience (a plus)
Extensive retail sales experience

Current knowledge of consumer market buying patterns and trends
Excellent communication skills
Degree in business or equivalent business experience

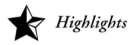 *Making the Cut*

Find a mentor with a successful product manufacturing company. Learn everything you possibly can. For those working within the beauty industry, begin now by marketing yourself as one who is the go to person for make up tips, new hair styles, healthy hair or whatever your niche may be.

Be a product guru who knows the features, benefits and ingredients of products. Study to discover how your product(s) can remedy a beauty problem.

 Highlights

Having your own products adds to one's credibility as a professional. There is potential in creating multiple branches to your brand such as "How to" books, videos and training materials. It can also lead to motivational speaking to encourage retailing and entrepreneurship.

@ *Tips*

LillyLabs.com
YourNamePro.com

2. BEAUTY SCHOOL OWNER

The Make Up

If there were no beauty school owners, many beauty industry jobs would not exist. Beauty schools prepare future professionals for various types of careers. Owning a school also provides career opportunities within the school organization: instructors, directors, customer service and admissions representatives.

Regimen

The owner's role changes depending on the number of school locations. Owners with 1 to 5 locations work closely with each school's personnel: directors, financial aid officers and admissions representatives. Larger school groups have additional layers of management who work directly with the team of school leaders. Owners attend conferences to make sure their schools are operating within federal and state guidelines, and to gain other information to help their organization. In addition, they assist in setting the budgets for each department. School owners are visionaries who plan and determine ways to better service their clients, the students. New training options such as online access, weekend programs, and other alternative learning methods are becoming popular.

 *Foundation*

High school diploma or equivalent
Five or more years of business management experience
Excellent problem solving skills
Salon and beauty industry experience (a plus)
Knowledge of school operations
Strong leadership skills

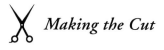 *Making the Cut*

Opening a school is a large investment. It takes years of planning and preparation. Find a mentor who owns a school or apply for a job as a school director or administrator. These positions will allow you to experience the school atmosphere and total business operation.

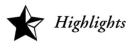 *Highlights*

Providing jobs for others, creating career paths and obtaining financial rewards are benefits to owning a school.

 Tips

Beautyschoolsdirectory.com
Beautyschooladvisor.com

3. BEAUTY SUPPLY RETAIL STORE OWNER

The Make Up

Retail store owners manage the total operation of products and services of the store. Retail stores that sell professional products have salons on site. Others sell non professional products although sometimes products are diverted (professional products sold in retail locations that are not approved by the manufacturer). Owners develop a customer base by researching and establishing their business in the best possible location. These stores are usually found in strip malls (centers) which make it convenient for area residents.

Regimen

When starting a supply store owners must be attentive to each area of the business. They decide what types of products and brands to sell. Employee training, inventory control, sales, promotions, customer check out and returns can all be the responsibility of the owner unless these duties are delegated to a store manager or employee. Owners work to establish a name within the community by carrying a wide variety of beauty products and tools, and through local advertising. Additional job duties include budget management, strategic planning, studying competition, reviewing customer needs and shopping trends.

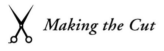 *Foundation*

High school diploma
Business degree (a plus)
Four or more years retail sales experience
Business management experience
Knowledge of beauty industry products and tools
Bookkeeping and accounting experience (a plus)
Good communication skills

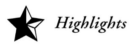 *Making the Cut*

Gain experience by working in a retail store part time or full time. It will help you to learn and to develop a system prior to making an investment. Look into partnership as an option and seek assistance in developing a business plan.

⭐ *Highlights*

Well managed stores in prime locations offer substantial financial rewards and the chance to open more locations.

@ *Tips*

Bizbuysell.com
Tannedfeet.com

4. CHILDREN'S FRANCHISE SALON OWNER

The Make Up

A children's franchise salon offers the freedom of owning one salon or a chain of salons with the support and proven system of a successful business chain. Children's salons have been revolutionizing the hair care industry for over a decade. It is a perfect hair care solution for kids and parents. Children's Franchise Salons can be theme designed and decorated, turning the salon experience into a child's retreat. Unique elements, along with customer training programs, help to create instant customer loyalty.

Regimen

The children's franchisee salon takes a sometimes very stressful and emotional hair care experience and transforms it into a fun filled family event. Franchisees oversee the hiring of a well developed staff of hair care professionals, implement marketing programs and help train the management staff. Owners also make sure that all bills are paid in order for the salon to operate properly.

 ## *Foundation*

Starting investments begin around $100,000, with minimum cash requirements of $50,000 and up.

In addition to the original investment, franchisees are usually required to pay annual franchisee fees starting at approximately $20,000. Royalties may also be paid.

Many franchise agreements require owners to commit to a minimum number of salon locations within a designated region.

Strong entrepreneurial spirit and drive

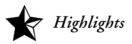 ## *Making the Cut*

Becoming a children's salon franchisee is a great opportunity for an entrepreneur with investment capital and a vision. Good credit standing, business management skills and knowledge of the beauty industry are other beneficial attributes.

★ *Highlights*

Opening a children's franchise salon can be a financially rewarding business investment. Also, the marketplace for children's hair salons is growing.

@ *Tips*

Snipits.com
Pigtailsandcrewcuts.com

5. CHILDREN'S SPA OWNER

The Make Up

Children's spas are popular business ventures. Chocolate facial masks and bubble gum pedicures provide a fun themed ambiance for the little clients. As an owner your vision sets the stage for the spa's brand, services, products and tools. Some offer dress up, fairy tale atmospheres while others are more centered around technology and education to teach healthy skin care practices. It is a popular birthday party spot for toddlers, tweens and teens.

Regimen

Train staff on techniques and company philosophy
Manage daily operations (opening and closing the spa, deposits and customer complaints)
Review daily retail sales and service reports
Develop marketing plans and strategies
Establish relationships with distributors

 *Foundation*

Licensed beauty professional (a plus)
Business management skills
Positive attitude
Problem solving skills
Strong leadership skills
Retail sales experience
Marketing experience

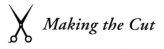 *Making the Cut*

Research the market and study other spa businesses. Take additional management, leadership and spa ownership classes to help prepare you for this business venture.

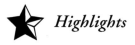 *Highlights*

There is opportunity to expand to additional locations for those whose concept works.

@ *Tips*
www.Greatwolf.com/Locations/Traverse/spa/scooopskidspa.aspx
Kidsspa.com

6. COSMETIC FRANCHISE OWNER

The Make Up

A cosmetic franchise owner typically operates their retail stores in mall locations, strip malls and kiosks. These franchise owners buy into an existing business that has a proven profitability track record. The Franchisor, parent organization, gives their franchisees support in all areas of the business: location, staff recruitment, technical training, operational management training, product knowledge, sales and marketing. Having a support system is a benefit to owning a franchise business.

Regimen

In the beginning it is important to work in your business as much as possible. Although you may be hiring a manager and staff to oversee the daily operations, one must be committed to the franchise to receive the maximum return on the investment. A daily routine may include: facilitating team meetings, reviewing bank statements, analyzing purchase orders, and solving problems that arise in businesses daily.

 *Foundation*

Licensed esthetician a plus
Three or more years of business management experience
Knowledge of current skin care and make up products
Excellent problem solving skills
Previous business education
Retail management experience (a plus)
Excellent communication skills
Strong leadership skills

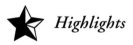 *Making the Cut*

Initial investments for cosmetic franchises may range from $50,000 to $200,000. There is an application process that determines if potential owners and the franchise organization are a good match; therefore it is important to extensively research all types of cosmetic franchise companies before beginning the application process.

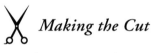 *Highlights*

Being your own boss
Opportunity to employ others
Being a part of a team
Continuous education for you and your staff

@ *Tips*

Franchisesolutions.com
Colormebeautiful.com
Merlenorman.com
Aloette.com

7. HAIR AND ACCESSORIES KIOSK OWNER

The Make Up

Beauty kiosks can be found in malls across America offering items such as ponytails, hair extensions, decorative combs, clips and other accessories. A kiosk offers the convenience of mall shopping to customers and foot traffic for owners. Kiosk owners rent a space and sometimes pay a set sales percentage to the mall.   Whether independently owned or franchised, becoming a kiosk owner offers outstanding growth potential.

Regimen

Recruiting and hiring staff to manage the daily operations is a primary job function. Researching product manufacturers and distributors is vital in determining the best possible products to purchase at an affordable cost and then retail to customers. Owners must also stay current with fashion and beauty fads to meet the wants and needs of customers.

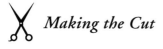 *Foundation*

Sales and retail experience
Entrepreneurial spirit
Previous management experience
Exceptional organizational skills
Analytical skills
Bookkeeping and accounting skills (a plus)
Negotiation skills

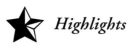 *Making the Cut*

Take business classes and gain hands on experience through retail management. Both will teach tools to effectively run a profitable business, to make good business decisions, to recruit the right staff, to market the company and to purchase the best products.

![star] *Highlights*

This is a great business venture for those who wish to run a retail business without the overhead expense of a full retail location.

Tips

Entrepreneur.com

8. HAIR ACCESSORIES MANUFACTURER

The Make Up

Start up capital and production costs are exceptionally low for small companies who wish to manufacture hair accessories.   Individuals, small companies and mega corporations produce millions of fashion trendy hair accessories each year.

Regimen

Whether you personally make the hair accessories or contract the production, each item needs to serve function and style. Constantly researching, designing and creating items for production will consume time; therefore having a team will be beneficial. Crafting the items with market appeal and uniqueness will increase sales.

 *Foundation*

Must be creative, and have an eye for design
Craft and artistic background (a plus)
Entrepreneurial spirit
Ability to sell and market designs
Retail experience
Business management experience
Negotiating skills

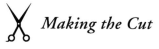 *Making the Cut*

Start with an inventory and research where to market and sell your products. If you want to know your product's selling potential, have a party and invite several people including stylists to test your products. Whether you are self employed or choose to work for a large manufacturer, you must have the craft skills and knowledge to design create and assemble a variety of accessories.   Here are some ideas on where and how to market your designs:
Internet stores
Consignment retailers
Mall kiosks
Small retail space in strip centers
Retail space in larger stores
Accessory and craft shows

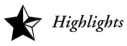 *Highlights*

You can be a hair accessory manufacturer wherever you live. This position allows you to have freedom to design and create unique items.

@ *Tips*

Longhairgirl.com
Goody.com

9. INDUSTRY MAGAZINE PUBLISHER

The Make Up

Industry magazines have educated the world of beauty for many years and continue to be a popular media to advertise and present new looks, techniques and trends. Magazine owners may decide to self publish when starting a beauty industry publication. Magazine owners/publishers work to establish a team of individuals who can work in the following areas: sales, marketing, graphic design, website development, public relations, writing, editing, photography and printing.

 *Regimen*

Magazine publishers strategically plan and budget funds for promotions, research, marketing and photo shoots. They oversee the sales team in securing advertisers for the publication and work closely with public relations firms and attend special networking events. Much time is spent negotiating prices with printers, advertisers and distribution companies.

 *Foundation*

Advertising sales experience
Marketing and Journalism experience
Four or more years of industry experience
Retail and product knowledge experience
Ability to build positive business relationships
Negotiation skills
Extensive knowledge of the beauty industry

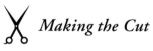 *Making the Cut*

Intern or take an entry level position with a fashion or hair magazine to gain experience. Next, develop a niche. There are many types of magazines. What will make yours different from the rest? After you've developed your niche, seek help from a mentor or consultant to develop a plan of action to secure funding and to operate the business.

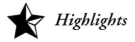 *Highlights*

You will form valuable partnerships, meet many other business owners and industry professionals.   This will open even more windows of opportunity.

@ *Tips*

Flipdog.com
Sixdegreesmag.com
Modernsalon.com

10. ONLINE BEAUTY SUPPLY STORE OWNER

♀ *The Make Up*

The internet provides the luxury of purchasing products by clicking a button. Online stores are becoming popular business ventures because they do not have high overhead costs incurred by on site supply store locations. This convenient source often referred to as e-commerce offers additional ways for established businesses to sell products and tools as well as opportunities for new businesses to develop their brand identity.

⏰ *Regimen*

Online store owners work closely with website developers and managers to improve the online shopping experience of customers. Marketing and advertising are also daily focus areas. It is imperative that plans are put in place to drive business to the website.

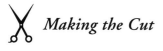 *Foundation*

High school diploma
Business degree (a plus)
Internet savvy
Knowledge of beauty industry
Excellent communication skills
Prior e-commerce experience

✂ *Making the Cut*

Investment capital for inventory is essential. Solid business relationships must be formed with suppliers to provide convenient, fast, safe and reputable service for online shoppers. Locate distributors, product and tool manufacturers that will support your needs and provide services for internet sales. Also take e-commerce classes, hold focus groups and shop online to conduct your own research.

★ *Highlights*

Internet jobs are expected to continue to grow over the next
few years.

@ *Tips*

Sallybeauty.com
Ohmybeauty.com

II. PRODUCT DISTRIBUTOR

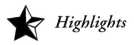

The Make Up

To become a distributor one must have extensive business
management and beauty retail sales experience. Distributors form
partnerships with new and existing product manufacturers to offer
professional products to local salons and individual operators. The
products are sold at discounted rates to provide a retail outlet for
professional brands. Distributors are local contacts and educational
liaisons for product manufacturers.

 *Regimen*

Job responsibilities cover a wide range of research on various brands. Consumer needs are analyzed to provide needed products and education. Merchandising, sales and consulting tools are taught to the sales representatives so they can assist salons with retail operations. Distributors hold local shows, classes, contests and other promotional events. They also provide avenues for professionals to obtain continued educational hours.

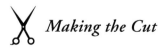 *Foundation*

Five or more years of industry experience
Five or more years of business operational experience
Business degree (a plus)
Detail oriented
Ability to establish business relationships
Team management experience
Excellent leadership and communication skills
Negotiation skills

X *Making the Cut*

This is a big commitment that requires many years of research, experience, dedication and knowledge. Warehouse and store presentation space may be required.   Apply for a job as a sales representative at an established distributorship to gain experience. Seek the help of a consultant, experienced mentor or other business professional to assist with creating a business plan. This will serve as a blue print for operating the company, provide a visual growth plan and determine start-up costs.

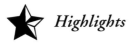 *Highlights*

Distributorships bring financial rewards and unlimited growth.

 Tips

Haircareproducts.suite101.com

12. SALON OWNER

The Make Up

Salon owners have diverse backgrounds. Some are beauty industry professionals: stylists massage therapists, manicurists, estheticians or others. There are also owners who have professional backgrounds in fields outside of the beauty industry. Both types of owners can bring positive and professional experiences and perspectives which can benefit the company.

Regimen

Owners who are licensed beauty industry professionals have the option to perform services and split their time between clients and managing daily business operations. Others focus specifically on daily operations including retail sales, ordering, customer service, loss prevention, merchandising, management, advertising, promotions and human resources. Owners strive to make sure each team member upholds the organization's mission and values at all time.

 ### Foundation

Licensed cosmetologist (a plus)
Previous salon management experience

Excellent customer service skills
Problem solving skills
Current knowledge of the beauty industry
Excellent communication skills
Retail sales experience
Effective time management skills

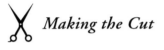 *Making the Cut*

Have a vision and be dedicated to achieving your goals. Do your research and make sure you understand what salon ownership entails. There's more to salon ownership than what you may see on the surface. Dig deep to see the true picture.

@ *Tips*

Stylecareer.com
Salondaily.com
Sba.gov
Irs.org

13. SPA OWNER

The Make Up

What makes a spa different from a salon? It's determined by the ambiance, philosophy and types of services offered. The spa owner is responsible for establishing a vision for the company, setting the tone and choosing the right people to be team members. There are many types of spas: day spas, resort spas, hotel spas, club spas and medical spas. Full spas are typically larger than the average salon and offer a wide variety of hair, skin care, nail and massage services.

Regimen

Owners work closely with spa directors to review goals and employee updates. Monitoring the marketing campaign, spa atmosphere, client experience, sales reports and other financial documents are all in a day's work.

 Foundation

High school diploma
Licensed beauty professional (a plus)
Current knowledge of spa features and benefits

Retail experience
Problem solving skills
Three or more years of spa management experience (a plus)
Strong leadership skills

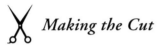 *Making the Cut*

Being a spa manager prior to stepping out into the world of entrepreneurship will help prepare you and set you up to flourish as a business owner. Thoroughly research various types of spas.

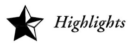 *Highlights*

Spa ownership often leads to opening more than one location. It is a retreat and creates a mini get-a-way for spa-goers, employees and owners.

 Tips

Experienceispa.org
Medicalspaassociation.org
Governmentguide.com

CHAPTER TWO
FREE TO BE YOU

Many hair stylists, make-up artists, students and other beauty industry professionals long to be freelance artists. Freelancing offers roads which can lead to both financial and creative freedom. Just think. Your creative work may one day be on the pages of *Vogue*, or it may be seen dancing across the stage of a Broadway production.

Live performances, commercials, TV shows, movies, the internet and other media also provide avenues to showcase your talents. Remember, the journey is not for the faint-hearted. Successful freelancers are resilient, highly skilled, determined individuals who will work 18 hour days for many consecutive months if need be. So, if you want to be free, get prepared, believe in yourself and make it happen!

*"I'd rather have huge success and huge failures
than travel in the middle of the road."*
Kevyn Aucoin

Diana Schmidtke
Male Groomer
Freelance Stylist

George Clooney, Will Ferrell, Ashton Kutcher, Kevin Costner, Ludacris, Harrison Ford, and Vin Diesel are just a few names on the star studded list of celebrities that Diana Schmidtke has groomed. As a freelance artist represented by the Celestine Agency, Diana has become a popular sought after stylist.

Like many aspiring celebrity stylists, Diana began her career working in a salon. After graduating from Pivot Point International Beauty School, she assisted the talented stylist, salon owner and colorist Phillip Palmeri. After fourteen months of training Diana's urge to break into the freelance market surfaced. She turned down the opportunity to work as a full time stylist in the salon and began her journey to freedom.

Diana proactively continued her education by attending all types of cosmetology classes: hair weaving, extensions, men's hairstyling, up do's, and cutting classes. This solid foundation gave Diana the spring board needed for her next big move.

At the age of twenty-two Diana relocated to Los Angeles with hopes of becoming a freelance hairstylist. After a few months of hard work, rejection, and disappointment she began working a "regular job." During this time Diana focused on her styling skills, studied the fashion, beauty, and entertainment industries, and continued networking. One day her big break came. She met a hairstylist who was represented by the Celestine Agency.

Although Diana soon landed a job assisting on photo shoots, she decided to move back to Chicago and rethink her plan of action. On a visit to Los Angeles, the hairstylist Diana met hired her to work with him on an advertising job. Diana blew him away with her styling ability, professional persona, and strong work ethic. He then introduced her to agents at the Celestine Agency. After six months of testing and putting together a portfolio, the Celestine Agency made the decision to bring Diana on board.

Now Diana travels all over the world working with celebrities, famous photographers, and peers doing what she loves. Because of her love for the industry, she has written a book entitled <u>SHORTCUTS To a Successful Career as a Hairstylist or Make Up Artist in the Fashion and Entertainment Industry.</u>

Diana encourages those who are interested in a freelance career to: "Take your time when choosing the right salon to work for. Be sure the salons have an excellent training program with assistants who have successfully completed the training program and are currently working on the salon floor. Take advantage of continuing education classes. A great artist is one who can learn something new from any peer. Personality determines your success in this industry. With hard work and the right people skills, I can assure you that you too will become a success."

Dianaschmidtke.com

14. BEAUTY AND FASHION WRITER

The Make Up

As a beauty and fashion writer your passion for the industry will influence hundreds of readers. This job allows one to interview top beauty and fashion idols, attend runway shows, be published in magazines and have the chance to review the latest in fashion and beauty products. You may choose to work as a freelancer or as a staff writer for a publisher, internet service or public relations group.

Regimen

Writers spend much of their time doing research and working to meet deadlines to complete: feature articles, product reviews, event reviews and news reports. There are many different writing avenues to explore as a beauty or fashion writer, and your daily routine will reflect your career choice. Writers read constantly to gain insight and to research subjects.

Foundation

Beauty industry professional (a plus)
College degree in journalism or related field (a plus)
Excellent writing skills
Four or more years of writing experience
Knowledge of current fashion and beauty trends

Marketing background (a plus)

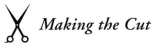 ## *Making the Cut*

Begin to develop your writing skills by taking classes, keeping a journal, volunteering your writing services and taking small writing assignments. Next, start a portfolio of your writing samples that have been published in news papers, magazines, periodicals and promotional material.

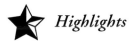 ## *Highlights*

Writing for the beauty and fashion industry is a fun job. If you write well and enjoy the beauty industry you can make a comfortable living in this position.

 ## *Tips*

Performancing.com
Essence.com
Lucy.com
Bridemag.com

15. EDITORIAL HAIR STYLIST

The Make Up

An editorial hairstylist is a freelance artist who is represented by an agency to work on various types of jobs. Editorial work is popular because of today's advertising demands. Companies and organizations market to many of their potential customers through print media. There are also countless numbers of publications that use fashion, portrait, beauty and lifestyle photography which are avenues for editorial hairstylists.

Regimen

Work with an agency to secure jobs
Assist other artists as needed
Continue to update your portfolio
Review tear sheets and attend meetings for shoots
Research styles
Listen attentively to the photographer
Work on magazine adds, catalogs, print marketing material, CD covers and web material

 *Foundation*

Licensed cosmetologist (a plus)
Three or more years of professional experience
Negotiation skills
Professional demeanor
Hard working
Persistent
Time management skills
Follow up routine
Professional styling kit

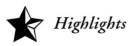 *Making the Cut*

You must work diligently to build a professional portfolio. It can take up to two years to create a solid portfolio. Network with other hairstylists, and look like a professional stylist at all times. You never know who you may meet on any given day. Finding agency representation may take time, but be persistent.

⭐ *Highlights*

Having your work published and getting the chance to work with celebrities is a benefit to this position. Building a name for yourself can help to market other ventures like salon ownership and product development.

@ *Tips*

Dianaschmidtke.com
Apparelsearch.com/models/hair_stylist.htm
Modelmayhem.com
Stocklandmartel.com

16. EDITORIAL MAKE-UP ARTIST

⧆ *The Make Up*

These artists are often represented by agencies, and work on multiple print and advertising jobs. Some agencies you search for may say modeling agency, but may actually represent make-up artists and hair stylists as well. There are also agencies that work exclusively with hair stylists and make-up artists. Freelance artists are usually paid a flat rate per job and pay the agency a percentage or fee for the booking.

⏱ *Regimen*

Work with agencies to secure jobs
Assist other artists as needed
Continue to update your portfolio

 *Foundation*

Licensed cosmetologist (a plus)
Negotiation skills
Professional demeanor
Hard working
Persistent
Professional make-up kit
Three or more years of professional experience

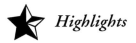 *Making the Cut*

Check out websites of great make-up artists. Also study photography. You may have great make-up skills, but if the photography is bad, no one will ever know how wonderful your work is. It is essential to know the difference between good and bad make-up as well as photography.

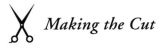 *Highlights*

Editorial make-up artists get discounts and can often receive sponsorships from major product manufacturers. Some choose to work for major brands as directors and educators while doing occasional freelance jobs.

@ *Tips*

Makeuphairandstyling.com
Elitemodel.com
Stocklandmartel.com
Kevynaucoin.com

17. FASHION STYLIST

 *The Make Up*

The goal of a fashion stylist is to capture the look, mood and vision of the photographer or director of TV, print, editorial or film media. They choose clothing, accessories and props of all kinds. Many work with agencies who book them just as a modeling agency books models for jobs. Some choose to run their own businesses and others may work for production companies, television studios, public relations firms, retailers and magazines. In addition, many fashion stylists have private clients who request their services for special events and public appearances.

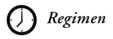 *Regimen*

Pull items for each job
Study fashion periods
Continually build a fashion portfolio
Coordinate looks
Place props

Foundation

Good credit standing
Knowledge of fashion history
Retail experience
Networking skills
Business management and follow up skills
Two year or four year degree in fashion design or merchandising
(a plus)

Making the Cut

Internships and apprenticeships are two paths that will help one to develop their fashion styling career skills.

Highlights

Wide range of job opportunities
Potential to work with celebrities

@ *Tips*

Allartschools.com
Fashion.about.com

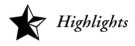

18. NEWS STATION HAIR STYLIST

The Make Up

This role incorporates hair styling for news anchors, guests and other correspondents. Many times a person is hired to do both hair and make-up if they are a licensed cosmetologist.

Regimen

Style hair and apply make up using up to date techniques which compliment the client's overall image. Stylists pull tear sheets (actual pages from magazines used for inspiration if styled by someone else or used in a stylist's portfolio as a sample of their work) and collaborate with wardrobe stylists. The goal for guests and anchors is to make sure each person maintains their personal style at all times.

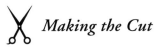

Foundation

Licensed cosmetologist
Three years of hair/make up experience "live" television
Excellent customer service skills
Ability to work flexible hours
Ability to work in a high pressure, fast paced environment

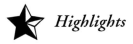

Making the Cut

Applicants should have references from other live television jobs. This may include assisting jobs and volunteering. Having a professional resume, portfolio and winning personality helps one to stand out.

⭐ *Highlights*

Many stylists move into TV and film as freelance artists. It is also gratifying to see your work on the news each day.

@ *Tips*

Craigslist.com
Timewarner.com
Job-search-engine.com

19. NEWS STATION MAKE UP ARTIST

The Make Up

This role helps to prepare news anchors, guests and other correspondents through the application of make up. Many of the artists work additional jobs while working for news stations.

Regimen

Apply make up using up to date techniques which compliment the client's overall image.

Foundation

Licensed esthetician
Three years of make up experience "live" television

Excellent customer service skills
Ability to work flexible hours
Ability to work in a high pressure, fast paced environment

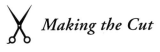 *Making the Cut*

Volunteer to assist other make-up artists and work for smaller live broadcasts around the community. Check the local paper and job search engines for job and volunteer opportunities. Working in retail will give one experience in make-up application and product knowledge.

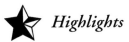 *Highlights*

Estheticians have the option to work for a salon or spa and others may choose to work on TV and movie productions as freelance artists or as an editorial make-up artist.

@ *Tips*

Monster.com
Craigslist.com
Check local news stations for available jobs.

20. MOTIVATIONAL SPEAKER

The Make Up

Motivational speakers move participants to take action by engaging them throughout the presentation. In the beauty industry speakers are hired for seminars, shows, school graduations, competitions and annual meetings. Speakers usually work independently and are paid per engagement. Some work for speaker's bureaus which act as a marketing representative and may request a percentage of the speaker's compensation.

Regimen

Writing material, studying industry trends, memorizing and perfecting speeches are job duties of motivational speakers. Those who get standing ovations, laughs, audience participation, and requests to return all have one thing in common. Practice!

Foundation

Excellent presentation skills
Five or more years of beauty experience
Ability to engage large audiences
Professional image

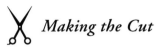 *Making the Cut*

Tone, inflection and pace are three ways to improve your speaking voice. However, there are many areas on which to focus to become an extraordinary motivational speaker including posture, movement, material and timing. Speak for free to develop your personal style. Talk about what you know. Don't fake it.

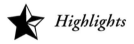 *Highlights*

Traveling to different places and motivating individuals to make a positive change in their careers and businesses is rewarding.

 Tips

Theexceptionalpresenter.com

21. PLATFORM ARTIST

The Make Up

Platform artists are highly skilled and perform at trade shows and industry events for hundreds of people. They teach and demonstrate the latest cuts, colors and styles to other professionals. Often, these artists work in a salon or barber shop, while also devoting other days including weekends to their stage careers. Vendors, distributors, and other beauty industry organizations hire platform artists.

Regimen

Performing demonstrations and presenting workshops while maintaining a clientele can be a demanding work schedule for a platform artist. They often compete in hair shows and contests, and devote many hours to training in order to master their skills.

 *Foundation*

Valid cosmetology or barbering license
Five or more years of professional salon experience
Licensure in multiple states (a plus)
Highly trained in specialty techniques
Advanced certifications: hair cutting, coloring styling and finishing
Industry competition experience
Outstanding stage presence

Excellent verbal communication
Professional body language

 *Making the Cut*

Having the knowledge, passion and confidence to perform under pressure are required characteristics of platform artists. Many times a stylist will work for a national company as an educator before performing on stage. This helps them to develop presentation skills. Working on a style team is also a great way to start your career as a platform artist.

★ *Highlights*

Freebies such as professional tools and products are occasional perks. They have the opportunity to meet and work with leading industry professionals. This job gives them a creative avenue to display their cosmetic talents.

@ *Tips*

Beautyschooladvisor.com/platform.jsp
Platformartistryuniveristy.com

22. RUNWAY HAIRSTYLIST

The Make Up

Fashion shows require a seasoned stylist to complete the designer's vision for a model's runway look. Most runway hairstylists are freelance artists who have worked in the editorial sector. Often designers request a key hairstylist who has a proven track record to work shows. Their job is to oversee a team of stylists behind the scenes of the show and to ensure that everyone understands the presentation's concept. Agencies are the best representatives to secure runway jobs.

Regimen

Runway hairstylists work with team members and take direction from the key hairstylist. This fast paced environment requires one to meet specific time constraints, to be technically creative, and to have the ability to produce quality high fashion styles. Stylists must also be familiar with hair extensions, wigs and styles from various time periods and the products used to achieve these looks.

 *Foundation*

Current cosmetology license
Agency experience
Professional demeanor
Excellent communication
Excellent listening skills
Time management skills

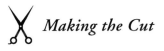 *Making the Cut*

Your portfolio and work ethic will help you to get agency representation. Return phone calls, emails and inquiries in a timely manner. Assisting to gain experience on photo shoots and fashion shows may not pay you monetarily in the beginning, but will pay off as you develop skills and network. You may find jobs posted online requesting that stylists work in exchange for prints, marketing opportunities and the experience of working for a show. Check local department stores, clubs and other organizations regarding local fashion shows, and volunteer to help other artists at trade shows. If you need to build a portfolio and want hands on training, bartering is beneficial.

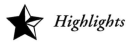 *Highlights*

If you love fashion you'll be living a dream as a runway hairstylist.

Those who   advance in their careers will work with remarkable designers and models.

@ *Tips*

Premiereshows.com
Style.com
Focusonstyle.com

23. TV AND FILM HAIRSTYLIST

The Make Up

Motion pictures and television could not make it without the touch of a fabulous hairstylist. Many times a cut and style can set the trend for millions of people around the world. Will you be that stylist who jump starts us into the next phase of beauty blitz? Hairstylists for TV and film are experienced professionals who have developed the service and technical skills required for this highly regarded position.

Regimen

Attend meetings

Review character images, designs and ideas
Prepare wigs, hair pieces, props, tools and products
Research hair styles from various periods for authenticity
Bring creative expertise each day
Be attentive on the set
Review and post tear sheets for visual references

 *Foundation*

High school diploma or GED
Licensed cosmetologist
Completed cinema make-up artist training
Excellent listening skills
Good communication skills
Effective time management skills
Current knowledge of beauty industry trends, products and tools

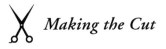 *Making the Cut*

The International Alliance of Theatrical Stage Employees Moving Picture Technicians, Artists and Allied Crafts of the United States (IATSE) has unions which represent make-up artists and hair stylists in the United States. They were originated to support the rights of make-up and hair artists working in film, television, network broadcasting television, commercial and theater. A union membership is necessary if you desire to work in these industries and be compensated appropriately.

To join a union there is a fee, and the applicant must have worked a specific amount of days on union projects. To work on a union project without being a member, generally you must be invited by a union member. Joining the union can be an arduous process. However, if you desire to have a career in film, it is definitely worth it.

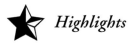 *Highlights*

Many hairstylists have been nominated to win Oscars for their award winning styles. In addition, those who work hard and are dedicated can make this a life long career.

@ *Tips*

If your state is not listed, contact the union closest to your residence and ask which branch represents your state.

Local 706	Los Angeles, CA	www. local706.org
Local 798	New York City, NY	www.iatselocalone.org
		www.798members.com
Local 476	Chicago, IL	www. iatselocal476.org
Local 488	Seattle, WA	www. iatse488.com
Local 13	Minneapolis, MN	www.iatse13.org
Local 665	Honolulu, HI	www. iatse665.org
Local 229	Denver, CO	www. iatse229.org24

24. TV AND FILM MAKE - UP ARTIST / CINEMA MAKE UP

The Make Up

TV and film often create characters whose make up requires extensive training and skill. Cinema make-up artists understand and are well versed in all types of make-up such as fantasy, high fashion, period, character, prosthetics, digital effects and special effects.

Regimen

Attend production meetings
Review character images, designs and ideas
Prepare working area, props, tools and products
Research subjects and periods for accuracy
Bring creative expertise each day
Be attentive on the set
See that make-up blends with the entire look of the picture

Foundation

High school diploma or GED
Licensed cosmetologist or esthetician
Cinema make-up artist training
Excellent listening skills

Good communication skills
Effective time management skills

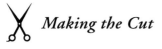 *Making the Cut*

The International Alliance of Theatrical Stage Employees Moving Picture Technicians, Artists and Allied Crafts of the United States (IATSE) has unions which represent make-up artists and hair stylists in the United States. They were originated to support the rights of make-up and hair artists working in film, television, network broadcasting television, commercial and theater. A union membership is necessary if you desire to work in these industries and be compensated appropriately.

To join a union there is a fee, and the applicant must have worked a specific amount of days on union projects. To work on a union project without being a member, generally you must be invited by a union member. Joining the union can be an arduous process. However, if you desire to have a career in film, it is definitely worth it.

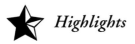 *Highlights*

Many successful make – up artists have been nominated to win an Oscar for their award winning performance. The work is considered an art form that contributes to the success of the movie.

@ *Tips*

 If your state is not listed, contact the union closest to your residence and ask which branch represents your state.

Local 706	Los Angeles, CA	www. local706.org
Local 798	New York City, NY	www.iatselocalone.org
		www.798members.com
Local 476	Chicago, IL	www. iatselocal476.org
Local 488	Seattle, WA	www. iatse488.com
Local 13	Minneapolis, MN	www.iatse13.org
Local 665	Honolulu, HI	www. iatse665.org
Local 229	Denver, CO	www. iatse229.org

25. WIG MAKER

The Make Up

Wig making is an art form. It takes technical precision, creativity and an enormous amount of patience. The theater, film industry and celebrities often request the services of a wig maker. Professional wig making fashions specific looks for clients that are uniquely made. The hair appears to be naturally grown by the person for which it was designed. Wig making has been around for centuries and continues to be in demand.

Regimen

True wig making is a lengthy process. First it begins with taking measurements, then creating a cast of the client's head and building a foundation using nylon netting. Following the initial steps is the needle work (knotting) process; this process is also called ventilating. A custom wig can take up to 40 hours or more to complete. Clients can pay up to $2,000 for a custom wig.

Foundation

Creativity

Patience and determination
Sewing skills
Excellent cutting, coloring and styling skills
Apprentice work or extensive wig making courses
Knowledge of film and theater industries

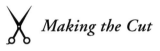 *Making the Cut*

Shadowing one who has worked for years and become a reputable wig maker will help you to master the techniques needed to create these works of art. If you are determined, put in the hours and attend wig making, cutting, coloring and styling classes.

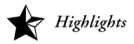 *Highlights*

Wig makers have a niche all to themselves, and often work with celebrity clients. They can see their work in productions on TV or in movies. Some receive awards for their creative work.

 Tips

Hairlineillusions.com

CHAPTER THREE
REACH AND TEACH

Education is a necessary variable in the equation of success. Our achievements are partly due to the wonderful teachers and educators who have devoted their professional lives to helping others learn. My cosmetology instructor used to say "Know that you know that you know." When I am preparing to speak or give a training session, I remember her advice and become less nervous. She truly made a positive contribution to my life by helping to shape my career.

Our industry offers a variety of ways to make education a career choice. Educators can work for a school, independent training company, salon, spa, manufacturer, distributor, or even start their own training organization. There are so many choices. Learn and explore the possibilities that education provides.

"We're so used to seeing beauty outside all around us here. I want everyone to come in and see the beauty inside these artists' souls."

Bobbi Brown

Teresa Lewis
Director of School Accounts
OPI Products, Inc.

Sixteen years working with the same company seems foreign to many in this day and age, but Chicago native Teresa Lewis has found career opportunities and longevity with OPI.

The path to a world of beauty emerged while Teresa was a teenager. At the age of sixteen she worked in a salon of a family friend who also owned a beauty school. While in high school, Teresa was so intrigued that she completed courses and became a certified nail technician.

Excited about career possibilities in the beauty industry, Teresa wanted to attend cosmetology school. However, under parental influence, she was compelled to attend college instead. She graduated with a degree in Accounting and immediately after graduation began applying at every beauty company in the Chicago area.

Teresa's career with OPI began as an educator. She managed a territory including Northern Illinois, Wisconsin and Iowa, and her passion for education grew as participants learned new concepts and had light bulb moments. "It is a feeling of accomplishment when an educator inspires a student."

As an account executive working with salons and sales

representatives, Teresa gained the insight she needed to be the Director of Schools for the Midwest region for OPI. Now she heads the OPI school division for the entire country. Teresa travels throughout the United States managing school accounts, programs, and nail educators to ensure that the quality, fun, and vibrant OPI brand continues to be a staple in the beauty industry for years to come.

Although a college degree is not a requirement for many of the positions at OPI, Teresa strongly believes in education. "Any education is good education. Just look beyond what you normally see. There's so much out there."

Finding licensed nail educators continues to be an obstacle for OPI and other companies.   " I think it is because they don't understand that the position is there. Many are in the salon, but if we don't go out and seek them, there just doesn't seem to be enough people period. People may get their license, but may not necessarily stick with the industry. You know, I never stuck with accounting. But if one is not interested in the salon, look in other areas within the industry: sales, education, marketing. There are other jobs available, but they may not be in the salon."

For information on becoming an educator for OPI,
go to OPI.com *or call* 800-341-9999.

26. ARTISTIC DIRECTOR

The Make Up

This technical position trains and develops cosmetologists and beauty professionals to reinforce efficiency, style and service. Artistic directors are responsible for regions (usually a few states) and normally work on educational teams. Chain organizations hire for this position.

Regimen

An artistic director is an experienced cosmetologist who often teaches daily seminars and workshops. These demonstrations require traveling to training studios throughout their assigned regions. Many times artistic directors organize national style teams and judge competitions.

Foundation

Valid cosmetology license
Master of fundamental and advanced cosmetology techniques
Excellent communication skills
Strong presentation skills

Detail oriented and organized
Willingness to coach support and train participants

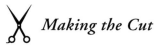 *Making the Cut*

Show initiative by being an outstanding team member. Take on a leadership role within the salon attending classes and shows and displaying excellent technical expertise. Work your way up by becoming a member of the design team, enrolling in competitions and volunteering for special projects.

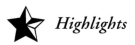 *Highlights*

Working as an artistic director is an outstanding career opportunity for people who have a passion for technical detail and giving excellent customer service. They are mentors who strive to develop teams that help salons within their region to be recognized as a quality brand.

 Tips

Supercuts.com
Regiscorp.com

27. BARBER INSTRUCTOR

The Make Up

Barber instructors work at barber or/and cosmetology schools that offer barber programs. They are licensed barbers who are experienced and have taken additional course work hours. They have also passed the instructor's exam required by the state in which they are working.

Regimen

Administer tests
Demonstrate techniques
Assist students with clinic services
Help with job placement
Prepare students for the state board exam
Assist students with contest enrollment
Coordinate field trips to shows, events, classes, stores, nursing homes and other businesses.

Foundation

Licensed barber

Current barber instructor's license
Two or more years of professional barber experience
Good verbal and written communication skills
Experience presenting classes and workshops

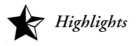 *Making the Cut*

Barbering is a profession with high standards. Instructors must exude professionalism and have a passion for education. Technology makes it easy for students to obtain information. Therefore, instructors must stay current on trends, techniques and tools used by platform artists, educators, barbers and stylists to teach students the proper way to service customers and build a clientele.

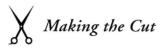 *Highlights*

A big reward is watching students achieve their goals. Many continue to work at a barber shop while teaching which provides supplemental income.

 Tips

Beautyschoolsdirectory.com
A2zcolleges.com

28. BEAUTY SCHOOL DIRECTOR

The Make Up

This position is located on the beauty school campus, and manages the operations of the school. This includes recruiting and hiring teachers, facilitating meetings, managing school expenses and maintaining the budget. Directors are also responsible for overseeing attendance, retention, clinic sales, maintenance requirements, and state board regulations. In addition they motivate, educate, and counsel students, teachers and admissions representatives on a daily basis. Directors must ensure that team members are educationally and professionally in the best possible position to effectively perform their jobs.

Regimen

A director's day usually begins early in the morning. Effectively planning the day makes this challenging job run smoothly. Review clinic floor retail and service sales, monitor class room operations, review enrollment leads with sales staff, prepare weekly reports for management, resolve customer complaints, maintain attendance percentages and monitor student retention.

 *Foundation*

Bachelor's Degree (some schools prefer a Master's Degree)
Minimum two years of management experience
Strong leadership and management skills
Excellent verbal and written communication skills
Proven track record managing budgets and analyzing profit and
loss statements
Must be organized and have exceptional time management skills
Sales management and or sales experience (a plus)

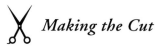 *Making the Cut*

This is a job for someone who has both strong administrative and
management skills. As the leader of a school you will have to conduct
performance reviews, interviews and may even have to reprimand or
fire someone. Directors must be willing to work long hours, know
the benefits and roles of each position within the school including
admissions, financial aid, instructing, clinic floor management and
career services. Excellent organizational skills and the ability to do
multiple projects while performing daily job duties are must haves.

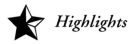 *Highlights*

Opportunity to develop others

Career advancement opportunities

@ *Tips*

Empire.edu
Monster.com
Beautyschoolsdirectory.com

29. CAREER ADVISOR

The Make Up

The advisor's role is to inspire potential, new and experienced professionals to stay in the industry, explore new avenues and maximize their talent. School organizations can utilize someone dedicated to job placement, goal setting, training and career advising. Career development makes a positive difference in helping students begin their careers as professionals in the industry.

Regimen

Build relationships with students to determine individual needs and aspirations. Coaching students individually and in groups, developing search skills, reviewing resumes, teaching interviewing techniques, and professionalism are daily job duties. Career advisors partner with local beauty industry businesses which will allow students to shadow and develop positive business relationships, obtain internships and jobs. They also work closely with teachers and administrators.

 *Foundation*

Five or more years of work experience within the beauty industry
Excellent networking skills
Bachelor's degree or equivalent work experience
Must have three or more years teaching or training experience
Exceptional organizational skills
Proficient computer skills
Extensive knowledge about career opportunities

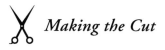 *Making the Cut*

Career advisors must have a passion for discovering beauty industry paths. They should also possess the ability to forecast jobs and trends.

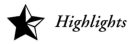 *Highlights*

Help shape the careers of future professionals,
Networking opportunities

@ *Tips*

Beautyschooladvisor.com
Uscollegesearch.org

30. CONTINUING EDUCATION TRAINER

The Make Up

A continuing educator teaches ongoing educational classes to enrich stylists in the cosmetology industry. Their classes range from cutting and coloring techniques to customer service and management strategies. Many state boards of cosmetology are requiring that stylists attend continuing education classes to renew their cosmetology licenses. As an educator, you support the course curriculum which is approved by the board in the state where you are teaching. Many times these classes are offered at beauty shows, trade shows and industry events. There are many ways to be employed as a continuing educator, you can be self employed, perform contract work, work for a salon, distributor or vendor. Being a continuing education trainer is a highly valuable asset to the beauty industry and a wonderful way to share your experience and knowledge with fellow beauty professionals.

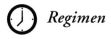 *Regimen*

Classes range from one hour to multiple day training events. Educators spend time creating detailed lesson plans and marketing their classes to licensed professionals.   They practice their teaching methods to improve class participation, consistency and topic information.

 *Foundation*

Training and education background, preferably in cosmetology
Valid cosmetology license
State Board approved class menu
Strong teaching and presenting skills

 *Making the Cut*

Attend classes for trainers that teach presentation skills and content development. It takes approximately five years or more to establish your credibility within the industry.

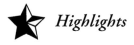 *Highlights*

The role of an educator has flexibility and is financially rewarding once you have established a class clientele.

Tips

beautytech.com/st_boards.htm

31. COSMETOLOGY EXAMINER

The Make Up

Examiners evaluate and supervise applicants applying for licenses in the beauty industry. This position will deal extensively with cosmetologists, nail technicians, and esthetician candidates. Many states hire individual examiners to administer the exams; however, some states opt to use an outside company to oversee the testing operations. If you are interested in becoming an examiner, check with your state board of cosmetology for guidelines and requirements. A list of cosmetology state boards is provided in the additional tips section.

Regimen

Grading and administering the practical performance examinations is a major job function of the examiner. It is important that all examiners are well trained and knowledgeable so that the best practices are used throughout the examination process. Most states require that examiners are not affiliated with beauty schools, and can not grade any candidates they personally know.

 *Foundation*

Must have a valid cosmetology instructor's license (barbering license where applicable)
High school diploma or equivalent
Be familiar with current terminology, methods and practices of cosmetology
Bilingual (a plus)

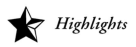 *Making the Cut*

Experience in the cosmetology field is required before becoming a state board examiner. Working in a salon or school to gain a strong understanding of practical procedures is a must. Management experience can certainly help your professional career in cosmetology. Remember that students and fellow cosmetologists count on state board examiners to be experts!

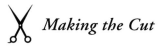 *Highlights*

You will be employed by the state in which you work. As a state employee you may qualify for their benefits package. Training is provided to examiners on an on-going basis to keep them up to date with requirements.

 Tips

Dlroope.com
Check with your state for examiner position information. Contact information for each state board is listed in the additional tips section in the back of the book.

32. COSMETOLOGY INSTRUCTOR

The Make Up

Cosmetology instructors work at beauty schools to help prepare students for a professional career within the cosmetology industry. They are licensed cosmetologists who have taken additional classes and exams to become instructors. Many times instructors are mentors to students and have a key position in shaping the careers of future professionals.

Regimen

Instructors facilitate both practical techniques and written course work.   Many schools have day and night classes which gives instructors an optional work schedule. Assisting students in finding jobs, providing feedback, grading assignments, participating in student shows and events, and managing classroom and clinic operations are among their many job duties. Some weekend work may be required.

 *Foundation*

Must be a licensed cosmetology instructor
Must possess two or more years of salon experience
Excellent problem solving skills
Good verbal and written communication skills
Experience presenting classes and workshops

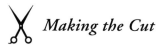 *Making the Cut*

Each school has a different look, feel and philosophy. However, they all have one goal in mind: to prepare students for a career in the cosmetology industry. I've interviewed potential instructors and searched for someone who not only had a passion for teaching, but also possessed a passion for learning. Know that you will learn as much from the students as they'll learn from you. Develop exceptional training methods and let interviewers know that students will be captured because of your interest and love for what you do.

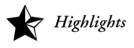 *Highlights*

A reward for this position is knowing that you're making a difference in someone's life. You may be the first person in the industry that a new student comes in contact with; make a great first impression.

 Tips

Beautyschoolsdirectory.com
Hairandbeautyjobs.com
Monster.com
Indeed.com
Spabeautyschools.com
Beautyschool.com
Beautyschooladvisor.com
Spabeautyed.com

33. DESIGN TEAM MEMBER

The Make Up

A design team member is selected for their exceptional skills and talent in cosmetology. Working on this team provides an avenue to showcase your knowledge, technical abilities and passion for the beauty industry. This group of highly skilled professionals is formed to support the company's overall commitment to quality. Many larger chain organizations have local, regional and national design teams for employees. This position is part time and requires that one be actively working in a salon.

Regimen

Companies structure the position in different ways. Often times, a design team member will work closely with the salon's staff to ensure excellence in service and overall quality. They share skilled techniques to help the salon's staff accelerate efficiency. Team members can compete in competitions, conduct workshops and assist management with recruiting.

 *Foundation*

Licensed cosmetologist
Two or more years of professional beauty industry experience
Strong technical ability
Professional presence
Excellent communication skills
Public speaking and presenting experience
Team player

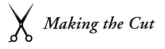 *Making the Cut*

Being selected to join a design team is an accomplishment. To be chosen from among your peers based on your skills, knowledge and preparation is an honor. If this is a career goal, be sure to prepare yourself by practicing your technical, communication and presentation skills.

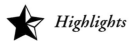 *Highlights*

Being a member of a design team is motivating and rewarding. This career opportunity allows your professional skills to shine. Additional training is given to team members which allows them to be on the cutting edge of style, fashion, trends and techniques.

@ *Tips*

Regis.com
CostCutters.com
ToniGuy.com

34. EDUCATION ADVISOR FOR SCHOOLS

 The Make Up

Larger school organizations employ education advisors to oversee the curriculum and implementation of teaching methods for their cosmetology and/or barbering programs. Advisors travel to national meetings and seminars to review materials and products presented by educational companies and vendors.

Regimen

Implement new training methods
Travel to schools to observe teacher training methods
Assist in conducting performance reviews
Approve lesson plan structure
Research and approve additional training material for schools
Manage continuing educational programs for teachers

 *Foundation*

Leadership skills
Licensed cosmetology instructor
Five or more years of teaching experience
Excellent communication skills
Good listening skills

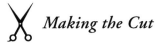 *Making the Cut*

Understand and believe in the company's philosophy.   Many organizations hire from within for this position.   Beginning your career as an administrator or instructor with a school will give you the training and decision making experience needed for this position.

 Highlights

Occasional travel
Helping to develop teachers

@ *Tips*

Beautyschoolsdirectory.com

35. EDUCATION EXECUTIVE

The Make Up

This position oversees the educational needs of beauty advisors within a major retail product line usually sold in department stores. Education is an important component that provides beauty advisors with tools to sell products and to service customers effectively. Through seminars, management training, and in-store training, education executives lead their advisors within a particular brand.

Regimen

Education executives are experts when it comes to product knowledge. They are the go to person for product features, benefits and additional selling and usage techniques. Coaching, developing and training advisors, managers and team members are additional job responsibilities. Developing and executing action plans, monitoring and promoting brand identity are additional responsibilities.

Foundation

Must possess excellent communication skills
Have a proven track record managing a team

Four or more years of sales experience
Extensive experience teaching and training

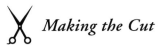 *Making the Cut*

High energy comes to mind when describing the person who will make the cut for this position. This position is for an educator who can motivate and inspire people to go the extra mile. Education executives must be able to create positive energy and enthusiasm about sales through training and coaching.

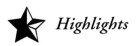 *Highlights*

If you like to teach, lead, coach and direct this is an ideal position. One will receive excellent continuous educational classes. What a fun and exciting way to learn more about the industry and help others.

 Tips

Esteelauder.com
Clinique.com

36. ESTHETICIAN INSTRUCTOR

The Make Up

An esthetician instructor teaches students the skills used to protect heal and beautify the skin. They create a learning climate of mutual respect and fairness that can encourage critical thinking and engage students. By enriching students with the latest trends, products and techniques of skin care, students will develop an understanding of the esthetic process.   To make esthetic programs more accessible, many students today look for non traditional teaching methods which may include: courses on the internet, cable television classes and self paced lectures, which all offer flexible class schedules.

Regimen

Demonstrate techniques to students
Assist with clinic clients
Administer tests
Help prepare students for the state board examination
Research trends and new techniques
Provide feedback to students
Maintain grades and records

 *Foundation*

Work experience as a licensed esthetician and/or cosmetologist
High school diploma or GED
Esthetician instructor's license
Prior training experience

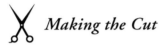 *Making the Cut*

Specialty certifications and degrees can boost your career as an esthetician instructor, such as medical esthetics, specialty spa treatments and advanced teaching credentials.

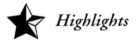 *Highlights*

Learn from leading beauty industry companies and trainers.
Develop skills to become a skin care expert

 Tips

Estheticianresource.com

37. FRANCHISE CONSULTANT

The Make Up

Franchise salon organizations hire consultants to provide support to franchisees, persons who own salons within the company. Many times franchisees do not have any experience in the beauty industry. I remember working with a franchisee whose previous job was being a chiropractor. Consultants help ensure the productivity and success of the salons. They also provide support in the following areas: management training, franchise orientation, store openings, team building, customer service, merchandising, theft prevention, service and retail sales.

Regimen

Consultants generally travel 90 to 95% of the time within their territories which can consist of a few states. Facilitating workshops can range from a two hour class to a two day workshop. When consultants are not teaching classes, they monitor salon operations, submit reports, draft recommendation letters, participate in shows, and make follow up calls. Franchise consultants also participate in quarterly meetings with other team members (marketing, finance, technical) and brainstorm on ways to better service the franchisees.

 *Foundation*

Bachelor's degree or equivalent work experience
Licensed cosmetologist (a plus)
Exceptional presentation skills
Excellent communication skills
Strong computer application skills
Well organized
Effective time management skills
Ability to travel 90% of the time

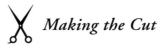 *Making the Cut*

Having a degree and a cosmetology license is a bonus when applying for this type of position. If you do not have a degree or do not plan to attend college, salon management experience is key. As a salon manager you'll learn many of the functions necessary to work as a consultant. These positions require one who is persistent and able to work effectively without much supervision.

 *Highlights*

One of the things that I liked most about this position was the travel. I was able to go to so many places and experience new adventures that I may have otherwise not been able to do. I absolutely loved the benefit of a company car and expense account. This position opened my mind to the vast number of career opportunities available within the industry. It also taught me valuable business and beauty industry information.

@ *Tips*

Regiscorp.com
Greatclips.com
Sportclips.com
Snipits.com

38. FRANCHISE OPERATIONS MANAGER

♀ *The Make Up*

Salon franchise organizations have a support system to help salons in the areas of marketing, technical, operational and finance. The franchise operational manager's role is to oversee trainers who provide educational classes and consulting services to franchisees and their staff. This person usually reports to an operations director and serves as a liaison between the corporate office and the salons.

Regimen

Operational managers help to train their team members in the areas of business management, employee development, team building, merchandising, retail sales and customer service. They also conduct performance reviews, assist with work calendars and schedule training sessions.

Foundation

Licensed cosmetologist or other industry professional
Prior management experience
Strong leadership skills
Good communication skills
Excellent time management skills

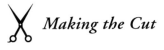

Making the Cut

Operational managers have proven themselves in the role of a franchise consultant. They have built positive business relationships with franchisees and have maintained positive results through their training and development efforts.

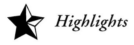 *Highlights*

As an operational manager, you help the careers of your team members. You are a mentor to many, including those working in the salon. Moving into a director's position is a logical step for promotion.

@ Tips

Regiscorp.com
Greatclips.com
Sportclips.com
Snipits.com

39. HAIR COLOR TRAINER

The Make Up

Usually considered an educational position, the goal of a technical trainer is to increase sales through product knowledge. Also known as technical advisors, trainers educate students and professionals about products, teach hair color theory, and demonstrate various color techniques. Hair color trainers are usually hired by manufacturers and/or distributors of hair care products.

⏰ *Regimen*

Trainers typically have a territory of a few cities and states, depending on the size of the organization. Classes are usually held at venues such as major trade shows, distributor workshops, and in salons. Many trainers work in the salon and teach classes part time.

Foundation

Must have a current cosmetology license
Three years of salon experience
Strong presentation skills with a charismatic personality
Extensive knowledge of hair color products and applications
Strong technical skills including cutting, styling and finishing
High school diploma or equivalent
Good driving record

✂ *Making the Cut*

Trainers are the stylists you see who are always changing their look. They always know which hair color placements best accentuate the haircut. They also know which colors compliment various skin tones. Sharpen your skills, volunteer to test products and techniques, and develop a positive business rapport with local distributors.

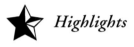 *Highlights*

The benefit of this position is the continuous inspiration trainers receive from educational classes. They also help other stylists to grow their hair color business. Trainers who excel within this position may have the opportunity to be promoted to platform artist, regional manager and artistic director.

@ *Tips*

Haircolorist.com
Also contact your local distributor and ask about becoming a hair color trainer or educator.

40. NAIL EDUCATOR

The Make Up

Even the experts take classes. That's one thing that successful people in the business of beauty products know. Continuous product education is important for the growth of these businesses. Product manufacturers hire nail educators to help increase sales through product knowledge and technical training classes. Educators teach various techniques and products to students and professionals. While some educators are full time, many are part-time employees for the manufacturer, and maintain a full time job as a nail technician.

⏱ *Regimen*

Nail educators teach classes at schools, distributor seminars, in salons, at sales meetings, trade shows, and manufacturer educational events. Travel is often times required, but is generally planned in advance. The number of classes educators teach depends on the size of their territory, experience level, and the market's need.

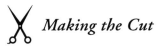 *Foundation*

Current nail technician license
Two years of professional experience
Knowledge of professional nail products
Team player
Excellent communication skills
Strong presentation skills
Positive attitude
Ability to build and maintain positive business relationships

✂ *Making the Cut*

You need to know all of the nail diseases by memory! Just kidding. You may want to brush up on them though. Educators have excellent communication, training and demonstrating techniques. They understand the history of nail art and are up to date with current colors, techniques and trends.

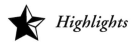 *Highlights*

Career advancement opportunities in the artistic and/or management arenas
Networking opportunities
Travel

@ *Tips*

Opi.com
Cnd.com
Nailpro.com

41. REGIONAL TECHNICAL MANAGER

The Make Up

Technical managers work for product and tool manufactures to ensure educators are well trained in product knowledge, techniques and trends. They oversee the markets assigned to their regional team members and travel to observe each person's teaching methods. They ensure that employee's skills are aligned with the organization's technical guidelines and procedures.

 *Regimen*

Schedule educational classes with regional team
Conduct performance reviews
Recruit and interview new technical educators
Help to create programs
Reward team members

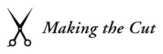 *Foundation*

Ten or more years of beauty industry experience
Leadership skills
Team player
Excellent communication
Current knowledge of industry trends and techniques

Making the Cut

Many times companies recruit technical managers by observing individuals within their organization that have proven themselves by being excellent educators. You can begin your educational career by working part time as an educator. Develop exceptional presentation and communication skills to compliment your vast product knowledge.

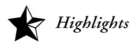 *Highlights*

Regional managers receive continuous training from top industry professionals. Many have the opportunity to travel to great places throughout the United States as well as internationally.

 Tips

Loreal.com

42. TECHNICAL SALON CONSULTANT

The Make Up

Franchise salon organizations hire technical consultants to provide support to franchisees, by helping salon managers and staff stay current with the latest trends, tools and techniques. Technical consultants also help with salon openings, team building, customer service and product knowledge.

 *Regimen*

Technical consultants manage a territory of salons and schedule workshops to meet the needs of the salons. Technical workshops include training on the following: hair cutting, new trends, finishing, styling and color techniques. Many salon organizations have design teams where stylists compete to travel to shows and events. Team members are selected to conduct seminars and to perform platform work. It is the technical consultant's job responsibility to oversee the selection process and training of the design team members.

 *Foundation*

Valid cosmetology license
Three or more years of salon experience
Experience teaching, coaching and/or training
Current knowledge of the latest technical tools and techniques
Positive attitude
Professional demeanor

Making the Cut

Technical consultants must have a strong background in teaching and training. They may have experience as an instructor, educator or team lead in a salon organization. Because technical consultants travel frequently, they must be well organized, dependable and have excellent time management skills.

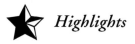 *Highlights*

Technical consultants receive excellent training and education from the leaders in hair care products and tools. Traveling to different academies shows and events are bonuses. They also receive free products and tools to test for marketing and training purposes.

 Tips

Regiscorp.com
Haircuttery.com
Toniguy.com

CHAPTER FOUR
THE SALON AND SPA EXPERIENCE

After graduation, the salon and spa experience is the best foundation for just about every position within the beauty industry. Working in a salon or spa environment teaches one how to truly give excellent service. It's not just about "My station." Salon services extend far beyond those given to clients. Stylists serve receptionists, managers serve stylists, owners serve employees, and the list goes on and on. Having extraordinary service, a warm ambiance, great products and an outstanding work ethic can spark positive word of mouth advertising and bring clients back for more.

"Repetition makes reputation and reputation makes customers."
Elizabeth Arden

Dennis Ratner
Founder and CEO
Ratner Companies

Ratner Companies is the largest family-owned and operated chain of hair salons in the country.   Dennis Ratner, a stylist, visionary and entrepreneur has built an empire with nearly 1,000 company owned salons, comprised of 4 brands including Hair Cuttery, Bubbles, Salon Cielo, and Salon Plaza.

"Many business plans are developed in boardrooms.   Ours was born on a cocktail napkin!" This brainstorming session happened over dinner in 1974 along with his partner Ann Ratner.   Since then, the company has provided thousands of career opportunities, provided quality service at affordable prices, and given back to the community through numerous charitable organizations and events.

Salons hold cut-a-thons to benefit individuals and special causes where 100% of the money is donated.   In addition the company's H.O.P.E. program – Helping Our People Evolve – matches stylists' fundraising dollars and provides grants to qualified stylists. Annually the company contributes $75,000 to the fund. Both locally and nationally, Ratner Companies gives BIG.   "My mission is to WOW and delight our stylists and clients, and I believe our commitment to charitable outreach is another way for us to do that everyday."

Dennis began his career in the beauty industry by working in his father's salon. This was his first job after graduating from high school. The work ethic and values he developed while working in the family business continue to be the solid foundation on which Ratner Companies is built.

Believing that the beauty industry provides unlimited opportunities, Dennis often shares his philosophy with students and professionals. "This industry not only allows one to make as much money a person wishes; it also gives one the chance to make a difference in the lives of clients by making them look and feel better. Just look what I've been able to accomplish with a positive attitude, a dream and a little hard work."

For information on career opportunities go to Haircuttery.com

43. AROMATHERAPIST

The Make Up

Aromatherapy is the science and art of using organic properties from natural substances, plants and essential oils in the holistic treatment of the mind body and spirit. Aromatherapists can work independently or in a spa. Using fragrance to promote clients' health and well being is the foundation principle. Aromatherapy is also used in chiropractor's offices and wellness centers.

Regimen

Conduct client consultations
Recommend product blends and treatments
Meet retail product sales goals
Explain benefits and features of essential oils
Demonstrate prescriptions for daily use

 ### Foundation

High school diploma
Knowledge of anatomy, physiology, essential oil extractions, botany and chemistry

Associate's degree in aromatherapy (a plus)
Exceptional customer service skills

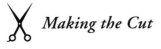 ## *Making the Cut*

Become an expert in the field by studying the science of aromatherapy, taking classes, volunteering and shadowing professional aromatherapists.

 ## *Highlights*

Like many jobs within this industry you can go as far as you want. International job opportunities are also available with this position.

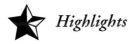 ## *Tips*

Hhnews.com

44. AREA SUPERVISOR

The Make Up

Franchise organizations and larger salon operations employ area supervisors who are assigned a specific geographical area. Their primary job responsibility is to oversee the operations of a group of salons. They report directly to the regional manager and are full time salaried employees. Depending on the organization, area supervisors may also be called district or general managers.

Regimen

Conduct store/salon visits within the assigned geographical area
Train and develop managers in operational
and technical procedures
Maintain weekly contact with managers through conference calls
Assist with recruitment and retention procedures
Review retail and service sales goals with managers
Review payroll and profit and loss statements
Prepare reports to be reviewed by regional manager
Attend home office meetings and trainings
Judge student competitions

 *Foundation*

2 or more years of management experience
Licensed cosmetologist (highly recommended)
Excellent leadership skills
Knowledge of retail sales, trends and products
Understanding of profit and loss statements
Ability to manage payroll and other business expenses

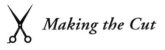 *Making the Cut*

Companies are looking for individuals who have displayed exceptional service as a salon manager, and those who understand total business operations. To make yourself more marketable, volunteer for special operational projects and take additional business classes.

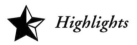 *Highlights*

Bonuses, international trips and a company car are benefits that companies may provide.

 Tips

Supercuts.com

Regissalons.com
Haircuttery.com
Smartstyle.com

45. ASSISTED LIVING HAIRSTYLIST

The Make Up

Many assisted living communities provide hair care services for residents and hire stylists to work full time and part time hours. There are also staffing services that provide stylists for nursing homes, health care facilities and assisted living communities. These businesses generally offer part time hours.

Regimen

Hairstylists provide routine salon services for residents: haircuts, chemical and styling services. Residents may also receive facials, waxing and nail care services.

Foundation

Current cosmetology license

Three or more years of professional experience
Excellent customer service skills
Positive attitude
Desire to work with senior citizens
Current knowledge of skin and scalp diseases and disorders

 *Making the Cut*

The right stylist for this position has experience working with people who may need special assistance and care. Showing stability on your resume through work experience and listing credible references will help job seekers.

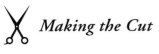 *Highlights*

Stylists in this position can truly make their clients' day. It is more than being a stylist. To many customers you become less like a stylist and more like a loving family member. Helping to put a smile on their faces will make you feel like you've just won the lottery.

 Tips
Indeed.com/forum/job/hairstylist

46. BARBER

The Make Up

The word barber is derived from the Latin word "barba", meaning beard. The profession has evolved over the years, and today barbers provide a variety of grooming services for men, women and children. Most barbers work in barber shops and can often be recognized by the striped pole. Many are independent contractors and others work based on commission (a percentage of the amount of services rendered) or a combination of hourly wages plus commission.

Regimen

Professional barbers shampoo, cut, style and color hair. They also provide beard trims, chemical and shaving services which makes the visit a one stop shop for many customers. Experienced barbers can service three or more clients per hour.

 ### Foundation

Professional licensed barber
Current knowledge of barbering trends and techniques
Product knowledge

Good customer service skills
Time management skills
Business management skills

 *Making the Cut*

Tighten up! All of your skills can be improved. Pay close attention to customer service, retail and technical skills. Remember, clients will return to you if you treat them well and only give them an average cut. However, if you give a great hair cut, and treat your customers poorly, chances are the customer will not return. In addition, they will tell others about their bad experience. Perfecting your service skills will help you grow a clientele and keep customers coming back.

⭐ *Highlights*

Many barbers become entrepreneurs either by owning a salon or renting a chair within a shop. Others branch out to become educators for clipper manufacturers and/or product companies. Becoming an instructor is also a popular avenue.

@ *Tips*

Indeed.com/barber
Beautybarbershow.com

47. BRAID SPECIALIST

The Make Up

Braid specialists perform a variety of braid styles for people of all ages. Locks, twists, corn rows, micro braids, tree braids and shreds are some of the popular styles and specialties. They can work independently by renting a station at a salon or by owing their own braid or natural hair care salon. Some specialists may work based on commission.

Regimen

Braiding services can take up to 8 or more hours depending on the type of style. Because of the length of time it takes to perform braid services, specialists generally work by appointment only. Also, some braid specialists work with assistants or other specialists to shorten the time of the service.

Foundation

Licensed cosmetologist
Ability to work long hours
Effective time management skills
Current knowledge of healthy hair care

Business management skills

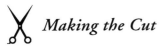 *Making the Cut*

Your work will speak for itself. Focus on your speed and communication skills to help increase your clientele. There's always a need for outstanding braiders who produce quality work and have great service skills. Take photos and submit your work to braid magazines to market yourself.

 Highlights

Specialists get to set their own hours. If you consistently market yourself, it can be a profitable business.

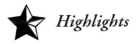 *Tips*

Afrohair.com
Hairboutique.com

48. COLOR SPECIALIST

The Make Up

Color specialists work in salons and specialize in an array of color services. Their extensive knowledge helps correct color problems, enhance moods, give younger appearances, compliment a client's look and accentuate haircuts and styles.

Regimen

Specialists work with women and men, and usually through appointments only. The consultation process is thorough to ensure the color service will match the client's life style.

Foundation

Licensed cosmetologist
Current knowledge of trends and techniques
Continued education in color classes
Certified color specialist (a plus)
Five or more years of salon or educating experience

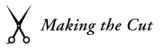

Making the Cut

Color specialists spend years training and developing their skills. Many choose to be educators for a specific color line to gain experience, to learn new techniques and to network with peers who have similar goals. Becoming an educator will add to one's credibility and allow a specialist to charge higher prices than other team members within the salon.

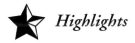

Highlights

Developing training materials, becoming a regional manger or director of education for a color line are potential career paths for color specialists.

@ Tips

Interhair.com
Behindthechair.com
Spabeautyed.com
Minardieducation.com

49. ELECTROLOGIST

The Make Up

Electrolysis is the process of permanently removing hair from the face and body using an electric current which destroys tissue. Private offices and salons hire electrologists as employees or contractors, and many operate businesses independently.

Regimen

The clientele base of an electologist includes both men and women. Women who have excessive facial hair are common clients of this service. Male clients often request their beards to be thinned and for other unwanted hair to be removed. Electrologists also shape eye brows and change hairlines. Generally they prefer to schedule appointments in advance. Often clients are scheduled for a series of sessions to achieve the best possible outcome.

Foundation

High school diploma or equivalent
Electrology Certification Program and License (check state guidelines)
Current knowledge of hair removal procedures
Good communication skills

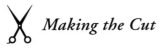 *Making the Cut*

The more training and education a person has, the more marketable he or she will be. To be hired by a salon, spa or electrolysis firm, take continuing education classes, attend shows and learn about new products and services.

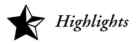 *Highlights*

Electrologists can move into teaching with training. Other career options include beauty counter management, make-up artistry, research and product development. If one wants to start an independent practice, initial costs are relatively low, starting under $10,000.

 Tips

Electrology.com/career.htm

50. ESTHETICIAN

The Make Up

Estheticians provide non medical skin care services to clients in a variety of settings: spas, cruise ships, resorts, medical facilities, electrolysis studios, hair replacement clinics, retail store cosmetic departments, brow bars and salons. They are paid hourly, based on commission or pay a rental fee for the space.

Regimen

Daily routines vary based on the needs of the clients. Here are a few services offered by estheticians: consultations, facials, body and facial waxing, eyelash and brow tinting, electrolysis, extractions, peels, and other facial and body treatments.

 Foundation

Must have a current state esthetician license
Excellent communication skills
Friendly persona and positive attitude
Be familiar with skin care products and procedures
Excellent customer service
Good organizational skills

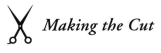 *Making the Cut*

Great estheticians are self motivated and excellent at marketing themselves. It doesn't take too much effort for those who really understand and believe that the services they offer can make a positive impact on a person's life.

 Highlights

Many estheticians have the ability to make their own schedules. Career opportunities include spa ownership, freelance make-up artistry and product development.

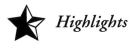 *Tips*

Beautyschoolsdirectory.com
Spabeautyschools.com

51. EYEBROW SPECIALIST

The Make Up

Well shaped brows can brighten a smile and even make people feel as though they've had a full makeover. For this reason, there is a high demand for great brow specialists. Brow specialists work in hair salons, spas, nail salons, make-up boutiques and brow bars. Many are self employed, while others work as employees.

Regimen

Brow specialists build a clientele just like hairstylists and other industry professionals. Established specialists who have developed their techniques can do as many as ten or more clients per hour.

Foundation

Current cosmetology or esthetics license
Excellent customer service skills
Good time management skills
Experience selling retail products

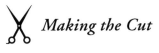

Making the Cut

One day I went to get my brows waxed and came back with only one eyebrow. If you're going to consider yourself a brow specialist, be sure you have mastered the art of shaping, not the art of shaving. There are various techniques to be mastered: waxing, threading, tweezing, reshaping, coloring and additional make-up tricks and trends. Work hard, study and become a true specialist. Most of all make sure that everyone leaves with two brows.

Highlights

For specialists who excel and are passionate about their profession, there is opportunity to work for specific product manufacturers including make-up and waxing lines. Some move on to develop their own products and tools.

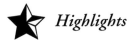

Tips

Anastasia.net
Check out amazon.com for books on eyebrow shaping. (*The Eyebrow* by Robyn Cosio, *How to Create the Perfect Eyebrow* by Victoria Bush)

52. HAIR EXTENSION SPECIALIST

The Make Up

Some people want hair enhancements for trend purposes, others want extensions to correct hair loss problems. Extension specialists are licensed cosmetologists who offer a variety of hair additions and lengthening services for clients. Some work independently servicing an extensive clientele. Others may prefer to work based on commission in a salon.

Regimen

Specialists conduct consultations to determine the technique that will be used, the type of hair and the style that will best suit the client's lifestyle. Methods include, infusion, sewing, quick weaving, braid extensions, and other variations.

Foundation

Licensed cosmetologist
Extensive knowledge of weaving and extension techniques
Continuing education classes
Excellent customer service skills

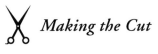 *Making the Cut*

A professional portfolio and excellent customer service will allow you to differentiate your services. Send your work to various beauty industry publications to increase your marketing exposure.

 *Highlights*

There is growth opportunity as an educator of a company that brands specialty techniques.

@ *Tips*

Hairextensions.com
Dazzlinghair.com
Bronnerbros.com/show
Premiereshows.com

53. HAIR REPLACEMENT SPECIALIST

The Make Up

Replacement specialists work in centers that provide non surgical hair replacement services. Non surgical hair replacement companies make hair pieces using human hair that are undetectable to most. The hair pieces are shaped and placed to cover any balding and thinning areas of the head. Replacement services have been popular for men throughout the years, and with new technology this service is appealing to a growing number of women.

Regimen

Consult clients on their overall look
Place and blend hair pieces with the client's existing hair
Cut and style hair pieces to suit the client's life style
Conduct follow up calls to guarantee customer satisfaction

Foundation

Licensed cosmetologist
Retail sales background
Excellent customer service skills

Well organized
Understanding of scalp diseases and disorders
Knowledge of hair therapy treatments
Strong technical skills (cutting, styling, chemical services)
Two or more years of professional salon experience

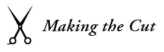 *Making the Cut*

Having a caring personality, professional salon experience, and strong technical skills will help one to obtain a position with a reputable organization.

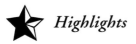 *Highlights*

Health benefits
Competitive salary
Continuous training

@ *Tips*

Hairclub.com
Ahlc.org
Scalpmend.com
Americanhairloss.org

54. HAIR STYLIST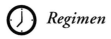

The Make Up

Stylists provide a variety of services that can enhance a person's overall look including: hair cutting, coloring, scalp treatments and massages, styling and chemical applications. You can walk into a salon and find that stylists are also motivational speakers, care givers and image consultants; their role is directed by the needs of the clients.   The profession has been around for years and is still in high demand. Salons are always in need of a professional, licensed stylist who is willing to learn and work in a team environment. Some salons pay stylists hourly or on a sliding pay scale which includes hourly pay plus commission. Others pay based on commission only (a percentage of the services). These options are good for new stylists. For experienced stylists with a substantial clientele (approximately 200 clients or more) booth rental is an option.

Regimen

Every day in the salon is different.   On any given day a stylist may do the following:
Conduct consultations
Make professional recommendations
Perform chemical services

Assist with cleaning duties
Maintain appointment calendar
Educate the customer on retail products
Shampoo, cut and style hair
Keep up to date customer records
Perform manicure and pedicure services (optional)
Perform waxing services

 ## Foundation

Must hold current state cosmetology license
Excellent customer service skills
Current on styles, trends, products and techniques
Retail experience (a plus)
Team player
Positive attitude
Willingness to learn

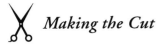 ## Making the Cut

It is important to find the type of salon that's best for you because there are numerous salon types. Visit at least five salons prior to making the decision to become a team member. Receiving a service or shopping for retail can give you a true picture of the salon's atmosphere and work philosophy.

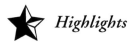 *Highlights*

Being a licensed cosmetologist can open so many doors for those who work hard to master their craft. Many of the jobs in this book only require a cosmetology license and a little experience in other areas. It is an industry where you can truly be yourself and one which encourages you to be as creative as you desire.

@ *Tips*

Behindthechair.com

55. MASSAGE THERAPIST

The Make Up

The practice of massage therapy dates back more than 4,000 years. Today, this scientific manipulation of soft tissues of the body is used for many reasons, including alternative healing, relaxation and communication. Achieving health and well being is the foundation principle for this popular technique.

Regimen

Massage therapy has evolved from not only using the hands but the fore arms, elbows, products and natural elements to accomplish massage techniques. Sessions are scheduled based on the needs of the clients and can range from thirty minutes to ninety minute sessions. Throughout the day therapists work with clients to address circulatory, muscle, back and stress related issues.

Additional services provided by massage therapists are: weight reduction consulting, exercise program recommendations, water therapy variations, dry heat treatments, ultra violet light treatments and infrared light treatments.

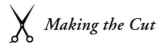

Foundation

Licensed massage therapist
Excellent listening skills
Great overall communication skills
Self starter
Member of a professional organization (a plus)

Making the Cut

Therapists must practice and take additional courses to master their techniques. Being professional, having a positive attitude, and exuding confidence will help you to secure the right job.

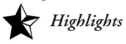 *Highlights*

There are many places to begin a career as a massage therapist. A few to consider are: medi-spas, cruise ships, sports teams, therapy centers and resorts.

@ *Tips*

Naturalhealers.com

Thrpy.topcareercshools.com

Massagetherapy.com

56. MOBILE SPA OR MOBILE MAKEOVER

The Make Up

Mobile spas bring spa services directly to clients. While it may be difficult to offer all of the services a regular spa may offer, mobile spas have succeeded by providing services that pamper and satisfy their clients. Common services include: facials, massages, manicures, pedicures, and body wraps. Conventions, corporate offices, parties, weddings, and special events are generally the target markets for mobile spa owners.

 *Regimen*

If you are working as a mobile spa employee, you may have the option to play dual roles. Some people moonlight by working at a salon or spa regularly, and work for the mobile spa only when booked for an event. Others are mobile 100% of the time. Large events could book your entire day, allowing you to work at one site location. However, smaller events can be spaced throughout the day.

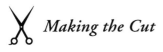 *Foundation*

Licensed massage therapist or esthetician depending on
services performed
Must be a team player
Self motivated
Business savvy – for those interested in owning their own mobile spa
distribution or company
Positive attitude

X *Making the Cut*

One must have spa and/or salon experience to win big in this position.

Learn all that you can about your craft by attending classes, shows and watching peers. Spending time developing unique customer service skills will help to separate yourself from the competition.

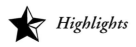 *Highlights*

Being in charge of your schedule, and also having the opportunity to become your own boss without the large overhead expenses of a typical spa is a huge advantage. This rewarding career allows one to help reduce stress and provide mini-get-a-ways for clients.

@ *Tips*

Mobilespa.com
Puurspa.com
Sparties.com
Mobilbeautysystems.com

57. NAIL TECHNICIAN

The Make Up

Nail technicians work in salons, day spas, medi spas, resorts, nail boutiques, fitness clubs, and on cruise ships. They promote nail care services and products to women, men and children.

(🕐) *Regimen*

Nail technicians consult with clients and perform requested nail care services for the hands and feet. They can perform services such as: sculpted or other artificial nail services, caring for the skin of the hands and feet, and massaging techniques to the arms, hands and lower legs.

 *Foundation*

Must be a licensed professional nail technician
Good customer service skills
Current knowledge of health and safety standards
Excellent time management skills
Retail product sales experience
Knowledge of current manicure and pedicure techniques

✂ *Making the Cut*

Learn to give quality services while effectively managing time. Nail technicians who master the marriage of quality service and time can build a large and loyal clientele.

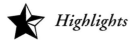 *Highlights*

Becoming an educator, entrepreneur, instructor or freelancer are options for nail technicians.

 Tips

Nailpro.com

58. REGIONAL MANAGER

The Make Up

A regional manager is a corporate position for a chain salon or privately owned multiple location salon organization. They are accountable for sales, services, payroll, and total salon operations. A regional manager is responsible for making the salon location and overall market profitable. This position serves as the liaison for site locations and the corporate office, and is essential in larger organizations to build relationships and implement systems to coach salon teams.

Regimen

Communication, communication, communication! Regional managers stay in constant contact with area supervisors to discuss location goals, normally holding weekly conference calls and individual meetings with managers. When not traveling to salons, regional managers work from a company office or from their home. They also travel to corporate meetings and national conferences.

Foundation

High school diploma or GED
College Degree (a plus)
Cosmetology license (a plus)
Five or more years of management experience
Outstanding leadership abilities
Team work ethic
Excellent communication skills
Experience working with profit and loss statements
Strong organizational and computer skills

Making the Cut

Regional managers work very hard to support and promote success in their regions. To land a position as a regional manager, you must display strong leadership qualities and have managerial experience, preferably in the cosmetology industry.

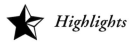 *Highlights*

Regional managers are often seen as assets to the organization and are promoted to other corporate positions.

@ *Tips*

Supercuts.com
Greatclips.com
Haircuttery.com
Jcpenny.com

59. SALON MANAGER & ASSISTANT MANAGER

The Make Up

The salon manager holds one of the most important positions within the salon organization. The success of the salon is directly related to how well the manager performs their job duties and responsibilities. Managers usually perform the duties of a regular stylist in addition to their management duties. Managers and assistant managers share many of the same duties. However, assistant managers generally do not conduct performance reviews, nor hire and fire employees.

 *Regimen*

Plan and direct salon operational activities
Manage to salon's budget
Review retail and service sales
Order products and tools for retail and back bar
Handle customer complaints
Conduct staff meetings
Manage salon cleaning duties
Conduct performance reviews with stylists and receptionists
Reinforce safety regulations, policies and procedures
Interview, hire and train new staff members

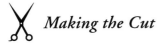 *Foundation*

Licensed professional
Knowledge of retail sales, trends and products
Understanding of profit and loss statements
Ability to manage payroll and other business expenses
Minimum six months salon experience (assistant manager)
Previous leadership role (manager)
Excellent customer service skills

✂ *Making the Cut*

Show initiative as a stylist to be considered for this position. Have outstanding attendance, volunteer for special projects, and mentor other team members.

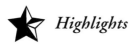 *Highlights*

Gaining management experience can help in career advancement goals. For example, opening a salon, becoming a manager or other beauty industry professional are logical career options.

 Tips

Beautyjobs.com

60. SALON COACH

 *The Make Up*

Salon coaches teach strategies and skills to assist in building successful salons. They provide encouragement, support and input for salon and spa owners, managers, directors and staff. Coaches give information, tools and resources for the salon to make business decisions and solve problems. Most salon coaches work for beauty industry training companies or work independently.

Regimen

Help set organizational goals

Motivate staff to implement and participate in programs
Provide and create educational resources
Teach operational workshops (management, marketing, retail, customer service and team building)
Give marketing strategies

 *Foundation*

Must have an established successful industry track record
Five or more years of experience as a licensed professional
Professional training and certification as a business/salon coach
Energetic personality

 *Making the Cut*

Many times working with professional product distributors can open doors for becoming a speaker at industry events which builds a platform for becoming a salon coach. Working in a salon or spa for several years to gain experience in daily operations will be a great start. Attend cosmetology and business courses to improve your skills. Just like coaching any team, it's valuable to be a player first!

⭐ *Highlights*

Salon coaches have a passion for the industry and enjoy sharing their experiences and knowledge. Being a salon coach offers job flexibility and career growth.

@ *Tips*

Saloncoaching.com
Salon-coach.com
Yoursaloncoach.com

61. SALON COORDINATOR

The Make Up

Spas and salons offer a variety of services including: microdermabrasion, acne treatment, Botox, treatment of spider veins, treatment of sun damaged skin, laser hair removal, skin rejuvenation, vein therapy, acne treatment and non surgical fat reduction procedures. Inside sales representatives or salon coordinators are hired to recruit clients and sell services to potential and existing customers.

Regimen

Follow up with clients to ensure satisfactory service

Conduct phone consultations
Network at local events
Interact with businesses, health clubs and non competitive spas
Develop sales techniques
Create customer service programs
Manage customer referral programs

 *Foundation*

College degree or equivalent work experience
Minimum one year of successful sales experience
Excellent telephone skills
Three or more years of beauty industry experience
Positive attitude
Great customer service skills
Ability to build positive business relationships

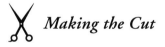 *Making the Cut*

Organizations want candidates to have experience and to be self motivated. The salon and spa environment is busy, so coordinators must be creative and flexible to effectively promote the organization effectively and see positive results.

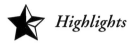 *Highlights*

There is an increasing amount of job opportunities in this industry. Coordinators often become salon coaches, consultants or salon owners.

@ *Tips*

Salonemployment.com
Salonjobs.com

62. SALON/SPA RECEPTIONIST

The Make Up

Salon Receptionists are often the first image of the salon. The person in this role should be energetic, welcoming and organized. This position requires excellent verbal skills, a high energy level, patience and a high understanding of salon and client services. Salon receptionists help the salon to run efficiently. This position will teach one about customer service, retail, business management and the salon industry.

Regimen

A salon receptionist greets clients in person and over the phone to facilitate the flow of appointments. Daily duties include: answering the phone, scheduling appointments, merchandising, welcoming clients, updating clients on wait times, making clients comfortable during wait times, assisting stylists with general salon duties and being a positive salon representative.

Foundation

Provide excellent customer service
Computer and cash management skills
Ability to multi-task and work in a fast paced environment
Knowledge of professional beauty products
Ability to schedule appointments effectively
Merchandising skills
Reliable and honest work ethic

Making the Cut

Working as a salon receptionist is a very versatile and valuable role in the salon.   Receptionists must be well organized and love working with people.

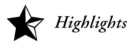 *Highlights*

Working full time for larger chain salons may offer benefits. Receptionists usually receive discounts on professional products. This position is also a foundation step for stylists, managers and salon owners.

 Tips

Behindthechair.com
Milady.cengage.com
Milady's Salon Receptionist Handbook

63. SPA DIRECTOR

The Make Up

The success of a spa is greatly influenced by the director who oversees the total operation of the company. While some directors have similar duties of a spa manager, many organizations give them job responsibilities that cover five major areas: financial, marketing, customer service, human resources and operations (sales, human resources and training).

⏲ *Regimen*

Spa directors are leaders within the organization who delegate tasks and understand the mission and growth forecast of the company. Planning strategically helps directors with other job functions like developing marketing strategies, reviewing financial reports, implementing programs, setting goals, solving daily problems and instructing managers.

 *Foundation*

Bachelor's degree a plus (not required)
Three years of spa management experience
Excellent communication skills
Strong leadership skills
Retail sales background
Knowledge of spa retail software
Excellent organizational skills
Experience working with budgets
Critical thinking and problem solving skills

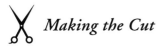 *Making the Cut*

Experience, professionalism, problem solving and leadership skills are key traits of successful spa directors. Many companies hire from within for this position. It is important to establish yourself with a company as a stylist, receptionist or other industry professional once you set a goal to become a spa director.

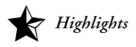 *Highlights*

Job opportunities as directors are increasing because of the growing number of new spas.

 Tips

Spatrade.com
Spafinder.com

CHAPTER FIVE
"BRAND" NEW IDEAS

Product, Price, Place and Promotion are the four P's that everybody learns when studying marketing. Simply put, marketing is the creative umbrella that moves people to purchase products, services and ideas. Shampoos, conditioners, hair sprays, flat irons, make-up, shows, events and seminars are only a small sample of products and services in the beauty business that require marketing expertise. If you have flair for coming up with new ideas and ways to brand them, know that there are jobs behind the scenes that may be just for you.

"Don't limit yourself. Many people limit themselves to what they think they can do. You can go as far as your mind lets you. What you believe, remember, you can achieve."

Mary Kay Ash

Nick Arrojo
**Stylist, Salon Owner,
TV Personality, School Owner,
Product Developer, Educator**

With a list of achievements behind his name the best is yet to come for super spectacular stylist Nick Arrojo. Maybe you've seen his hair work on TLC's What Not To Wear, or perhaps you've witnessed him on stage demonstrating his signature razor cutting techniques. If you have not had the privilege to be engaged by the art of Nick Arrojo, put it on the top of your "To Do List."

As a teen, Nick began his career at a salon near his hometown, Manchester, England. He quickly developed a passion for the industry and landed an apprenticeship at Vidal Sassoon. He took full advantage of the educational programs there and found the team learning atmosphere refreshing and motivating. " I learned about precision hairdressing, creative expression, and that you're only as good as your last client."

Nick's commitment to hard work began to pay off early on in his career. Vidal Sassoon awarded him the Young Hairdresser of the Year at age twenty-one. He soon became the youngest Assistant Creative Director ever hired at the company. After a decade Nick became a leading educator as the Creative Seminar Leader for Wella, United Kingdom.

In 1994 he moved to New York and worked as the Director of Education for Bumble and Bumble. Today, juggling roles as owner of

Arrojo studio, cosmetology school and product company, Nick still finds time to perform as Artistic Director for Wella. Internationally, the Arrojo team travels to beauty shows teaching techniques and trends to audiences of up to 4000 people. Nick and his staff work diligently to manage his businesses. He has had phenomenal growth, expanding his salon to 40 stations and incorporating an advanced education facility. "I firmly believe the progress comes down to our hard work, team ethics, and commitment to excellence."

Encouraging future, new, and seasoned professionals is also a passion of this entrepreneur. He believes in professionalism, mastering one's craft and doing the right things for clients. "Have strong focus, plenty of ambition and strive to be the absolute best. Find a hair salon where the focus is on the team. You can learn from the people around you and use experienced stylists as mentors. Team centered salons are also likely to have a structured training program. Absorb all of the education you can, especially in the early part of your career."

Nick Arrojo's commitment to education and dedication to his career goals shows that being a hairstylist is a high-end career for those who want it to be. " The most successful stylists have many strings to their bow and can get a job anywhere in the world. Remember, you can work in education, fashion, editorial, film, television or theatre."

The most important lesson Nick has learned over the years, "To be professional. The more professional we are as hairdressers the more respect we'll get for the work we do."

64. BRAND MANAGER

The Make Up

Most major product manufacturers hire brand managers to market their products and business image. Brand managers in the beauty industry ensure that a particular product or line looks, feels and is designed to match the overall creative vision of the company. Managers execute marketing plans and programs to increase brand awareness and maintain consistency throughout the product's life cycle.

Regimen

Responsibilities of managers include conducting a SWOT (Strengths, Weaknesses, Opportunities and Threats) analysis of the products. The SWOT analysis is a report that analyzes the organization, competition and market environment. It helps brand managers manage the brochure creating process, discuss strategies for local and regional marketing, track competition, develop new plans, manage and create new products.

Foundation

Bachelor's Degree in Marketing, Master's Degree (preferred)

Must have a strong interest in beauty products
Three or more years of marketing experience
Possess strong leadership skills
Excellent communication skills
Self motivated

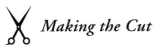 *Making the Cut*

Start in an entry level position with a vendor. Branding incorporates the product as well as the culture of the organization. Companies want managers who understand this concept and someone who can develop new brands which will be a reflection of the company's mission, goals and values.

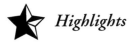 *Highlights*

This role is a key position within the marketing department of major product manufacturing companies. It is exciting and allows one to see their hard work on the shelves of major retail stores, salons and spas.

@ *Tips*

Careerbuilder.com
Loreal.com
Monster.com

65. DIRECTOR OF INDUSTRY RELATIONS

The Make Up

This is a senior level executive position within chain organizations. These directors work diligently to promote cosmetology as a career choice, and serve as public relation specialists for the company's brand. They also represent the industry as a lobbyist at the national level to ensure current issues and industry needs are communicated.

Regimen

The daily function of a director of industry relations can change from day to day. This career is full of travel, corporate events, legislative work, board meetings, conference calls, networking, and research. Building strong working relationships with cosmetology schools, product manufacturers, distributors, industry professionals, associations and other organizations is also an essential responsibility. Directors speak at trade shows and various industry conferences throughout the year to promote their company, give business and industry updates, and educate business leaders on governmental procedures and guidelines. Their national sponsorships, public relations and advertising efforts fertilize the recruitment and retention of salon employees at regional and local levels.

 *Foundation*

High school diploma
College degree
Extensive management experience
Superb networking skills
Exceptional level of understanding of the cosmetology industry
Outstanding communication skills
Excellent presentation skills
Strong organizational skills

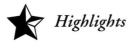 *Making the Cut*

A director of industry relations is typically hired from within an organization and has shown themselves worthy of the position through hard work in management, team building and leadership. They believe that cosmetology is a viable profession and encourage others to help make more opportunities become available for future professionals.

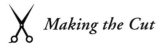 *Highlights*

This position leads to other executive and consulting positions.

@ *Tips*

Regiscorp.com
Greatclips.com
Careerbuilder.com

66. MANNEQUIN STYLIST

The Make Up

Beauty supply stores sell synthetic and human hair for those who like to change their look. Hair manufacturers send mannequin heads which are cut and styled with various types of hair for in store displays. The stylist's job is to present current styles to entice customers to purchase the hair. This position is usually done on a part time basis with the option to move into a full time position as an educator and representative for the manufacturing company. Working in a department store styling clothing, accessories and hair for mannequins is also an option.

Regimen

Test hair by placing wefts onto the mannequin. Give feedback to the manufacturer on items that are defective. Create styles that are current and practical for the target market of the product line.

 Foundation

Licensed cosmetologist
Current knowledge of industry trends and techniques
Strong technical skills
Effective time management skills

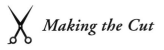 *Making the Cut*

Begin by building a professional portfolio of styles using hair extensions. Create a diverse book using models of different ages, and looks. Research various hair product manufacturers to check for job opportunities.

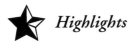 *Highlights*

As a mannequin stylist you influence style and fashion for hundreds of people through your creative expression of hair styling.

@ *Tips*

Macys.com

Sensationnel.com
Domehairs.com
Jcpenny.com
Dillards.com

67. MERCHANDISING SPECIALIST

The Make Up

Merchandising specialists work for major product manufacturers and travel to salons and retail locations to display retail products which create sales appeal to clients and customers. This position is for licensed and non-licensed beauty professionals.

Regimen

Specialists work closely with retail associates, managers and staff to educate and promote retail sales. They follow plan-o-grams (blue prints for displaying products) to maximize selling potential.

 *Foundation*

College degree (a plus)
Salon experience
Successful record in retail or merchandising
Professional image
Ability to analyze sales trends

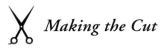 *Making the Cut*

Your resume should meet all of the foundation requirements and list work experience in retailing and merchandising.   Although organizations train specialists it is important to have prior training.

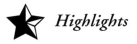 *Highlights*

Being a merchandise specialist is a great career. You will also have flexibility in your daily routine.

 Tips

Craigslist.com
Monster.com

68. ONLINE BEAUTY CONSULTANT

The Make Up

An online beauty consultant advises clients on beauty services and products. Consultants can sell products through an online retail store or by having a combination of stores linked to their blog page or website. One can also work as an independent consultant for a major brand that offers e-commerce services. Many consultants begin working on a part time basis.

Regimen

Provide online consultations
Offer suggestions on hair care services
Provide a photo gallery of options for clients
Provide virtual makeovers and tours
Give advice and guidance for specific events: weddings, proms, anniversaries
Sell products and tools online

Foundation

Licensed cosmetologist or esthetician (a plus)

Knowledge of beauty retail products
Ability to form business relationships with online store
owners and vendors
Computer and internet savvy
Strong selling skills

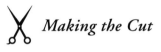 *Making the Cut*

If you want to be an independent beauty consultant build a clientele base by working with multiple retail stores, marketing and promoting your consulting services for special events as listed above, and working with clubs and social organizations.

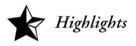 *Highlights*

This job can be done from anywhere in the country. The internet has and will continue to provide flexibility in jobs. Make sure that this job is not a conflict of interest with your current full time position.

@ *Tips*

Marykay.com
Governmentguide.com
Avon.com

69. R & D HAIR COLORIST

The Make Up

A research and development hair colorist tests, analyzes, and helps to find ways to improve products for major hair color manufacturers. Usually this position works with a team that is passionate about creating the best possible hair color products for stylists and consumers. Some companies require that research and development stylists work in their on site salons in order to monitor the products, process, timing, and outcome.

Regimen

One's daily routine may include servicing clients in a salon environment while using various color products. In addition, stylists must be able to determine potential problems, suggest improvements, and give general salon feedback.

Foundation

Licensed cosmetologist
Extensive background in hair color
Five or more years of professional experience

Exceptional customer service skills
Outstanding communication skills

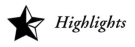 *Making the Cut*

As you begin your career as a stylist, start forming positive business relationships with local product distributors. This is an easy task because many product sales representatives stop by salons regularly. Let them know that you want to volunteer to test new products. This will help to give you practice in providing helpful product usage feedback. Keep a record of educational classes and certifications that you've earned throughout your career. Educational information should be added to your resume to show your enthusiasm for learning new styles and techniques.

★ *Highlights*

Many hair color manufacturers offer full benefits for their employees. Classes from top industry professionals and occasional travel may also be an added benefit.

@ *Tips*

Pg.com
Monster.com

70. REALITY TV SHOW CONTESTANT

The Make Up

There are many reality television shows that capture the attention of viewers each week. Our industry provides an avenue for the competitive edge of stylists to be seen in homes across America. A reality TV show contestant is an industry professional who works full time and fits a particular show's criteria.

Regimen

Shows generally request that contestants temporarily leave their current full time position while filming. Contestants usually do not receive money unless they win the entire contest or win a specific round on the show. They perform various industry related tasks and compete with other beauty industry professionals.

 Foundation

Licensed industry professional
Extensive salon and/or spa experience
Competitive spirit
Unique personality
Willingness to work on a team

Self motivated
Job flexibility

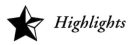 *Making the Cut*

Be persistent and research specific shows. You can contact the network directly through their website to find out about casting calls, rules and regulations. It is competitive on the show and just as competitive to be selected for the show. Be yourself and let your personality shine.

⭐ *Highlights*

Shows can bring national exposure which can help to boost a person's career. You will also have the chance to get advice from leading industry professionals. Winners have substantial financial rewards.

@ *Tips*

Showhype.com
Realitytvmagazine.com
Bravotv.com

71. SALON AND SPA MARKETING MANAGER

The Make Up

Marketing managers help to develop the overall brand of the salon. The brand or company persona should be properly presented in all forms of advertising: yellow pages, web pages, radio, newspapers, magazines, television and special promotions. Marketing managers help salon owners to secure the best rates and spots for advertising campaigns. The goal is to help salons and spas increase traffic flow and sales through public relations, planning, research, advertising and marketing. Marketing managers work for franchised salon organizations, industry marketing companies, and independently.

Regimen

Work with salon owners to implement a marketing plan which outlines the marketing promotions and advertising for the year. For example, holiday specials, sales, gift card promotions, seasonal discounts (prom, Mother's Day, Father's Day), newspaper, radio and TV spots.

Foundation

Degree in business or equivalent work experience

Thorough knowledge of the beauty industry
Ability to establish long term business relationships
Effective organizational skills
Three or more years of business marketing experience
Previous work with radio, TV and print media
Negotiation skills

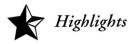 ## Making the Cut

Ideal candidates are leaders and are able to show salon owners the benefits of effectively marketing their organization. Marketing managers must spend time researching the industry and studying the strategies of the salon's competitors.

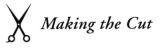 ## Highlights

Marketing managers get to see the results of their hard work quickly. They help and watch businesses become more profitable and establish a recognizable brand within the community.

 ## Tips

Careerbuilder.com

72. TRADE SHOW MARKETING COORDINATOR

The Make Up

Have you ever received a hair show brochure in the mail? Perhaps you've seen posters in salons or beauty retail stores. One of the people in charge of these forms of advertising is the marketing coordinator. They are the contact person for advertising, direct mail and other marketing pieces for hair shows and events.

Regimen

Coordinators work closely with other team members within the show organization. They collaborate closely with graphic artists and the organization's president to produce marketing pieces that encourage show participation at all levels.

Foundation

Degree in business
Trade show experience is a plus
Excellent communication skills
Strong organizational skills
Ability to meet deadlines
Previous experience working with advertisers

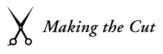 *Making the Cut*

Having a marketing vision and displaying attention to detail will help one to secure this position. Previous beauty industry experience can also benefit potential coordinators.

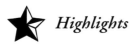 *Highlights*

Meet and work with hundreds of beauty industry companies and organizations. This type of marketing experience can lead to promotions from within as well as outside of the organization.

 Tips

Ibsnewyork.com
Premiereshows.com
Americasbeautyshow.com

73. TRADE SHOW OPERATIONS COORDINATOR

The Make Up

Going to beauty industry trade shows is an exciting event where one can purchase products at discounted rates, learn about product knowledge, see the stars in action, and learn key concepts to help move you to the next level. This position is located at the show office headquarters. Operations coordinators work closely with the show president, sales, and exhibitor services to secure sponsorship for events. Coordinators also manage and book all travel and hotel arrangements for events. In addition, they also work as a liaison between the show group, travel companies and hotels.

Regimen

The day in the life of an operations manager includes making calls, managing emails and following up with companies to ensure that event locations and travel itineraries are secure. Scheduling speakers and trainers for trade show education is another important role of coordinators. Having a positive rapport with all third parties is essential to making sure the events operate smoothly and commitments are secure.

 *Foundation*

Bachelor's Degree in Communications or Marketing
Excellent computer skills: Microsoft Word, Excel and Power Point
Experience in trade shows and events
Must be well organized
Proactive problem solving skills

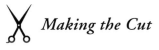 *Making the Cut*

Working in the beauty show business is exciting yet demanding. Understanding the goals of the organization and being able to effectively manage multiple projects will help you to land this type of position.

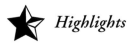 *Highlights*

Working for shows and events is fun, and affords the chance to learn a wealth of knowledge about the beauty industry both technically and operationally.

 Tips

Ibsnewyork.com

Premiereshows.com
Americasbeautyshow.com

CHAPTER SIX
FOR SALE

A major element of the beauty industry is sales; however a frequent comment from many salon professionals is, "I'm not a sales person." Sales is about educating clients and making professional recommendations. We should all realize the importance of sales; it is the heartbeat of our industry. Record sales in products, services and tools are what keep our industry in high demand. For those who recognize their selling potential and are intrigued by the beauty of sales, this section is for you. For everyone else just peep inside and see what's "for sale".

"If you don't sell, it's not the product that's wrong, it's you."
Estee Lauder

Judy Rambert
Education and Research
Vice President
Pivot Point International, Inc.

Judy Rambert's mark on the industry can be found in beauty schools all across the country. As Vice President of Education and Research for Pivot Point, Judy oversees the development of training materials for students, teachers and trainers. Judy became interested in the beauty industry after she went to a local cosmetology school to get her hair styled. "I was watching and was amazed at how much fun it seemed to do other people's hair." At the age of eleven she wanted to be a hairstylist.

At the end of her sophomore year in high school, Judy entered into a cosmetology program. Soon after finishing the program, she began working at a salon. Her thirst for knowledge led her to Illinois State University where she majored in business. However, while in school she discovered that something was missing. "I missed being behind the chair." Consequently Judy began to work at a campus salon near by. "I worked on Saturdays and a couple of days a week. It was good money."

Not only did Judy work as a stylist for many years, she also became a licensed cosmetology instructor. Because of her husband's job, they moved frequently. "The beauty was that each time we moved, I was able to find a job quickly. It is wonderful that we have an industry that allows us to combine different skill sets, desires and wishes to do things and remain connected to the industry." By the age of 28, Judy had ten years professional experience and began her career with Pivot Point.

Judy's years of hard work and education did not go unnoticed. After teaching haircutting and design she was asked to move into the publishing division to help the team create the _Scientific Approach to Hair Sculpture_. The publishing division of Pivot Point creates course books, text books, DVDs and CDs. She enjoyed creating educational content for the company and was later promoted to be Educational Director of the Publishing Division. In her current role of Vice President of Education and Research, "I get to work with people who have doctorate degrees in education and great people in our education, editorial and graphic design divisions. We identify a prototype and work with publishing to create it. In turn we look at how to teach our trainers these programs and the best delivery methods. For example, if we create a long hair course we look at the mannequins that will be used, the length of the hair, the density of the mannequin and the hair color."

The rise to the top has led Judy on an amazing journey that continues to allow her to help thousands of students, teachers and other industry professionals. Her passion for the industry encourages her to continue her education while running Pivot Point's new Education and Research division.

"Surround yourself with people who are interested in education and are always learning. Stay motivated. We have a very caring profession where people like to share information. The more you know, the more you can share. Continue to network with others; opportunities and doors will open up which can take you on an amazing journey in this industry."

74. ADMISSIONS REPRESENTATIVE

The Make Up

Beauty industry schools hire admissions representatives to increase
student enrollment. Representatives work at the school and are
typically full time employees. They are the initial point of contact
for potential students and are required to represent the school in the
most professional manner possible. It is a fast paced position that
requires one to meet deadlines and goals on a daily basis.

Regimen

Calling prospective students and setting up appointments are major
job duties of admissions representatives. They formally introduce
students to a career as a beauty industry professional. Representatives
also meet with school directors and sales managers weekly, prepare
reports and maintain a rapport with students and teachers to improve
recruitment and retention.

Foundation

Bachelor's Degree (a plus)
Background in cosmetology (a plus)

Excellent communication skills
Two years of sales experience
Phone etiquette and follow up skills

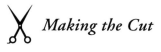 *Making the Cut*

Sales experience and the willingness to learn about the beauty industry can help one to attain a job as an admissions representative. References are also valuable.

 Highlights

This position gives incentives to representatives who reach and exceed goals. It is rewarding and can lead to career advancement opportunities within the company.

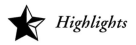 *Tips*

Empire.edu
Beautyschoolsdirectory.com
Paulmitchelltheschool.com

75. BEAUTY ADVISOR

The Make Up

Typically beauty advisors are employed by both the retail store where they work and the product brand they represent. Responsibilities include: meeting daily sales goals established by management, learning product benefits and features, and demonstrating excellent customer service skills.

Regimen

Being a beauty advisor includes working in a team environment. If you like meeting new people and have a love for beauty products, this may be the job for you. A daily routine may include mini makeovers on clients to entice customers to purchase moisturizers, lipsticks, shadows, and other beauty products. By giving extraordinary customer service and the occasional sample freebie, one can build positive relationships with clients.

Foundation

Excellent communication skills
Friendly personality
Excellent customer service skills

Knowledge of beauty products and application

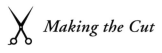 *Making the Cut*

A smile goes a long way! Believe that if you get the interview, you can get the job. Your confidence and uniqueness should win them over. Show that you're interested in the product line, job duties and enjoy working in a team environment. A large portion of this job is sales, so if you make the sale in the interview, then you'll do well on the job.

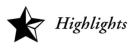 *Highlights*

Networking opportunities! In this position one can meet people from all walks of life, including TV news personalities, celebrities, photographers, fashion designers, and others related to the beauty industry. There is also opportunity for those who show interest to move into management or freelance opportunities with the retail line.

 Tips

Esteelauder.com
Clinique.com
Bobbibrowncosmetics.com
Monster.com

76. BEAUTY INDUSTRY SOFTWARE SALESPERSON

The Make Up

This job may seem extremely high tech, but if you can use a self check out machine at a grocery store, then you can probably understand the software concept used in salons and spas across the country. These programs help salon owners and managers with routine salon and spa operations. Having a software system is a necessity to effectively conduct and manage successful businesses.

Regimen

Much of a salespersons job is educating clients. There are various options to help new clients as well as existing ones learn how to utilize each function of the salon and spa software. Online classes, on site training, telephone training, and group workshops are different ways to reach prospective clients and maintain existing software users. Salespersons also participate in tradeshows to create awareness and to recruit new clients.

Foundation

Effective negotiation skills
Two or more years of sales experience

Excellent computer skills
Good communication and organizational skills
Beauty industry experience
Self motivated
Team player
Positive attitude

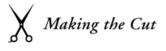 *Making the Cut*

Organizations who hire for these types of positions are looking for someone who has a proven track record in sales. These people have the ability to develop positive business relationships and understand the operational needs of salons, spas, retail stores and outlets. The salesperson must also be a visionary.

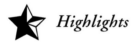 *Highlights*

In this position one can learn the importance of scheduling, data tracking, and sales reports in the daily operation of salons and spas. This position provides opportunity to travel, to network, and to learn how to run a successful beauty business.

 Tips

Harms-software.com
Prosolutionssoftware.com

77. BEAUTY SERVICE REPRESENTATIVE

The Make Up

Have you ever purchased a product and needed help with the application process? Perhaps you know someone who may have had an allergic reaction to a product. Call centers for major product manufacturers handle concerns by hiring customer service representatives to direct calls from physicians' offices, customers, and others who call with product and distribution questions and concerns.

Regimen

Service representatives work as a team to answer inquires. Their goal is to respond to customers promptly and to address their concerns effectively. Daily job duties include: entering orders, returning calls, directing and handling customer complaints, opening new accounts, following up on distribution, recommending products and analyzing reports.

Foundation

Excellent communication skills

Bachelor's degree (not required by all companies)
Detail oriented
Team player
Experience in customer service
Knowledge of beauty industry (a plus)
Pleasant phone etiquette
Computer savvy

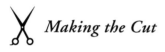 *Making the Cut*

It's all about your customer service experience and the interview. Make sure that you have met the qualifications for the company and do well in the interview.

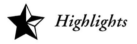 *Highlights*

Many call centers offer flexibility; both part time and full time jobs are available. The team environment is fun, and like many of the positions in this industry call centers provide stability.

@ *Tips*

Monster.com
Indeed.com

78. BEAUTY STORE SALES ASSOCIATE

The Make Up

Customer service and retail sales are the primary functions of beauty store sales associates. They typically work shifts of 4 hours or more and are paid hourly.

Regimen

Associates assist clients with purchases and returns. Associates recommend products, tools and services and also help provide options. Helping with in store promotions, merchandising, and inventory are other daily job responsibilities.

Foundation

High school diploma or equivalent
Good customer service skills
Positive attitude
Ethical and honest work habits
Ability to work nights and weekends

✂ *Making the Cut*

Companies like to hire people who will be dedicated. It is costly to recruit and train employees. Your schedule and goals should meet the needs of the store.

★ *Highlights*

Learning product knowledge will benefit individuals who may later want to pursue career options like: cosmetologist, educator, sales representative or manager.

@ *Tips*

Craigslist.com
Sallybeauty.com
Ulta.com

79. BEAUTY SUPPLY STORE MANAGER

The Make Up

Store managers are responsible for coaching employees, in store promotions, inventory control and customer service. Their role is important to the overall success and profitability of the store. They work to achieve sales goals and customer satisfaction. Most supply store managers are salaried employees or are paid hourly wages.

Regimen

Make sure employee's scheduled work hours do not exceed the standard payroll budget. Conduct inventory and place orders for products and tools. Receive shipments and check items with purchase orders. Assist employees and handle customer and operational problems that may occur throughout the work day.

 ### Foundation

High school diploma
Two or more years of retail and merchandising experience
Strong leadership skills
Ability to multi-task
Ability to work long hours, holidays and weekends

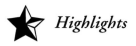

Making the Cut

Show initiative by having consistent work experience on your resume. Store owners want managers who are eager to learn and willing to go the extra mile to get the job done.

Highlights

Managers with a successful record are in high demand. For larger companies managers who excel may move into regional management positions.

Tips

Sallybeauty.com
Ulta.com

80. COSMETIC ACCOUNT COORDINATOR

The Make Up

Coordinators are employed by department stores and represent an assigned vendor line. They oversee the vendor account at designated stores within their territory. Working to achieve financial goals, the role of this position observes and coaches team members at each location.

Regimen

Cosmetic account coordinators are liaisons for the buying office, vendors and stores. They give recommendations based on their observations of team members and feedback from visual merchandisers, counter managers, cosmetic department managers and store managers. Implementing programs and special events also help them to drive sales of the brand. They lead by example, displaying techniques to attain sales goals, extraordinary service, productivity and a team environment.

Foundation

Four year college degree or equivalent work experience
Prior retail management experience

Proven leadership skills
Energetic personality
Excellent customer service skills
Ability to travel
Ability to work flexible hours
Analytical problem solving skills

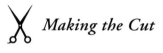 *Making the Cut*

Employers always want to hire the best person for the job. Make sure that you have a solid foundation. Obtaining this position requires enthusiasm for selling retail. It is a high energy atmosphere and demands one to perform multiple tasks. Your resume and personality should reflect all of these characteristics.

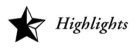 *Highlights*

Advantages surround those who excel as cosmetic account coordinators. Management positions with vendors or department stores are logical career paths. The sales, management and marketing experience gained from this position can be used in various career paths within the industry.

 Tips

Neimanmarcus.com

Nordstrom.com
Macys.com
Bloomingdales.com

81. COSMETIC BUSINESS MANAGER

The Make Up

The cosmetic area is one of the most vibrant departments of a store, and generates major sales revenue. Cosmetic business managers work for large chain department stores, and oversee sales associates of multiple brands. They ensure all cosmetic sales associates and counter managers continually strive to achieve departmental goals.

Regimen

Business managers are leaders who work on the retail floor but have additional responsibilities. These managers teach methods to grow the client base, interview, recruit, review productivity and promote brand awareness. Other daily operational duties include: selling and product training, building partnerships with vendors, emphasizing selling techniques, motivating the staff, and assisting with merchandising.

 *Foundation*

Cosmetic and beauty industry knowledge
Prior sales experience
Must be goal oriented
Experience working in a busy environment
Good communication skills
Positive attitude
Team player

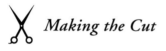 *Making the Cut*

A positive attitude, strong work ethic and experience as a counter manager or advisor will help you to secure this position.

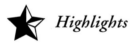 *Highlights*

This position can lead to an upper level management position.

 Tips

Macys.com

Nordstrom.com
Dillards.com
Yahoohotjobs.com

82. COUNTER MANAGER

The Make Up

Beautiful ribbon tied boxes, unique bottles filled with fragrances and vibrant shades of shadows glow on the counters of department stores all across the country. Working diligently behind the scenes is a person who is an asset to the retail operation. Counter managers ensure that the retail sales are up, customers are satisfied and that sales associates are driven and customer friendly.

Regimen

A daily routine may include setting sales goals for associates, recruiting candidates and training employees. Interviewing and hiring the right staff will help to make the counter manager's job easier. Management is a rewarding position, but can be tough if the right people are not in place. Managers conduct performance reviews and support their team while motivating them to achieve goals.

 *Foundation*

Excellent communication skills
Management experience
Ability to recruit, hire, and train candidates
Merchandising skills
Must be organized
Proactive problem solving skills

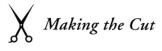 *Making the Cut*

Counter managers are team leaders. One must have experience in managing or operating within the role of a manager on special projects and events. Meeting and exceeding sales goals regularly will show management that you are ready for this type of role. Regular attendance at work is a plus. Managers often time work long hours and sometimes work shifts for absent employees. So make sure that you're up for the challenge. It's a wonderful opportunity to learn, grow and become an extraordinary leader in the beauty industry.

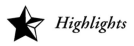 *Highlights*

This high paced environment can prepare managers for upper level management positions.

@ *Tips*

Macys.com
JcPenny.com
Yahoohotjobs.com
Monster.com

83. FRANCHISE SALES REPRESENTATIVE

 *The Make Up*

Beauty industry franchise organizations hire sales representatives to create growth opportunity within the organization by selling franchise agreements. Driving expansion is a primary goal for franchise organizations and need in order to have longevity, increased market share and brand awareness.

Regimen

Representatives generate sales leads for a specific region or territory by networking, attending trade shows, and monitoring industry trends. They make recommendations to management on potential franchisees and assist prospects throughout the agreement process.

 *Foundation*

High school diploma or equivalent experience
Must be an effective negotiator
Excellent communication skills
Extensive sales experience
Must have experience managing accounts
Professional demeanor

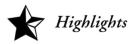 *Making the Cut*

Franchise sales representatives drive franchise organization's market share. Sales representatives must have previous sales experience, overall knowledge of the benefits of franchise ownership, and be able to negotiate and close sales.

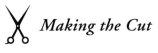 *Highlights*

This position offers full benefits including vacation, medical, dental, and health. For representatives who excel this position's salary and incentives are highly competitive.

@ *Tips*

Careerjet.com
Gethairjobs.com

84. TERRITORY SALES MANAGER

Q *The Make Up*

As a territory sales manager you will represent one or more product lines which may include: human and synthetic hair, hair accessories, beauty products, hair color, styling tools, equipment, and more. This is a sales position that requires one to travel approximately 95% of the time. Clients are generally other beauty businesses including salons and retail stores.

⏲ *Regimen*

Daily you will interact with customers as well as staff members. The driving force behind this position is sales education, influencing most territory managers to be goal oriented. Building relationships and educating clients on products and or services is the key to being successful in this position.

 *Foundation*

Must have approximately three years sales experience
Ability to manage customers within a region (usually a few states)
Excellent time management skills
Possess knowledge of the beauty industry
Prior salon experience (a plus)
Proficient in Microsoft Power Point, Excel, and Word.

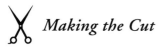 *Making the Cut*

One must have the ability to solve problems on their own. There's no one there standing over your shoulder micromanaging you. One must show confidence and convey that through time management, organizational, communication and sales closing skills you will be able to meet the expectations of the company.

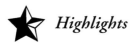 *Highlights*

Many companies pay territory sales managers a base salary plus commission. This means that the commission you make is a reflection of the amount of business obtained. These positions may also offer full benefits including vacation, health and dental insurance, and a retirement savings plan.

Tips

Monster.com
Careerbuilder.com

CHAPTER SEVEN
DREAM, CREATE, EXPLORE

The "beauty" of the beauty industry is that there are multiple jobs available for the multi-talented individuals who make up the industry. Every stylist, make-up artist, massage therapist, nail technician, barber, teacher, educator, student or other beauty industry professional that I have met seems to have many talents. Some people think that you should find one thing that you like, do it well, and stick to it. I beg to differ. If you have the gift of doing more than one thing well, then do all of them. Make a plan and use all of your gifts and talents. Training and education will help you to master them.

"I had to make my own living and my own opportunity. But I made it!"

"Don't sit down and wait for the opportunities to come. Get up and make them."

Madam C. J. Walker

Your Beauty Mark

_____ Name

_____ Future Career Title

When did you first become interested in the beauty industry?

_____

_____

_____

_____

_____

_____

_____

_____

Describe your ultimate career goal. Be specific. _____

_____

_____

_____

_____

What educational classes are needed to achieve your ultimate career goal? When will you complete these requirements?

_____

_____

What is the best advice you have received about achieving your career goals?_____

_____

_____

_____

_____

How will you make a positive impact in the world of beauty? _____

_____

_____

_____

_____

_____

85. ASSOCIATION MEMBERSHIP SERVICES REPRESENTATIVE

The Make Up

Associations are non profit organizations that provide resources and events for members. They also provide industry tools to help businesses and individuals prosper. Information on licensing requirements, business trends, operational and technical procedures for schools, salons, beauty companies and professionals is essential for excelling and moving to the next level. Professional beauty associations operate by offering memberships and membership packages. Membership service representatives serve as resources to potential and existing members.

Regimen

Representatives assist in explaining the benefits of the organization and other related concerns. Through association events, networking and research, they help to grow the organization. Because the staff of associations is relatively small, project development and project management are additional job duties.

Foundation

High school diploma

College degree (a plus)
Project management experience
Excellent communication skills
Ability to build positive business relationships
Public speaking ability

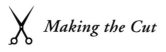 *Making the Cut*

This position is one of service which requires a person to have a positive attitude. Ideal candidates should enjoy working with people and believe in the mission of the organization. Make sure your values are aligned with those of the association.

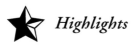 *Highlights*

This role can lead to key project management jobs within the organization and with other industry companies.

 Tips

Ncacares.org
Salons.org

86. BEAUTY EDITOR

The Make Up

If you ever flip through a magazine and look at the masthead, you'll see the names of editors and others who make up the staff. Many magazines targeted towards women, men and teens have beauty editors to make sure the beauty stories and photographs appeal and speak directly to the magazine's target market.

Regimen

Beauty editors work closely with art directors, writers and photographers to discuss new ideas, shoot concepts and current news. Researching story ideas for magazine beauty sections, editing copy, cover trade shows, special events and press events are additional job duties. Responsibilities may vary depending on the size of the organization.

 ### Foundation

Degree in journalism, related field or equivalent work experience
Experience writing and proofing articles
Management experience (not required by all)
Attention to detail

Project management experience
Proficient using various types of computer software programs
Ability to discover new talent

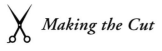 *Making the Cut*

Fashion, style, celebrities and the latest trends inspire beauty editors to do their jobs. Having the ability to produce quality work will help a person to be more qualified for this position. Writing experience, helping the team execute photo shoots, and covering events will groom one for a position as a beauty editor.

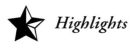 *Highlights*

This job is demanding, but filled with glitz and glam. Networking at major events, meeting celebrities and testing the latest products are perks to this job. Major magazines offer full benefits.

@ *Tips*

Essence.com
Allure.com

87. COSMETIC CHEMIST

The Make Up

New cosmetic products hit the market frequently: lip gloss, nail polish, facial scrubs, glitter, perfume and more. Cosmetic chemists have a passion for exploring and researching. They are hired by product manufacturers and have extensive experience in research and development.

Regimen

A cosmetic chemist spends time in the lab, mixing, testing and researching the exact formulas to make beauty products that are useful, safe and appealing. These chemists formulate ingredients that make shampoos, conditioners, perfume, lotion, make up, scrubs, body sprays, colors, perms, styling and finishing products.

 *Foundation*

Laboratory research experience
College degree in chemistry
Knowledge of product development
Understanding of the beauty industry and cosmetics

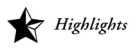 *Making the Cut*

There are certification programs in cosmetic chemistry that take a year or two to complete. Many have graduate degrees.

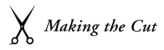 *Highlights*

This is a steadfast research position that creates the products that make up the beauty industry.

 Tips

Society of Cosmetic Chemists - Scconline.org

88. COSMETIC REGISTERED NURSE

 *The Make Up*

A Cosmetic Registered Nurse (RN) is responsible for providing professional nursing care to patients. By assessing, planning, implementing and evaluating the care of patients these nurses are beneficial to plastic surgeons and dermatologists. The field of skin care, plastic surgery and medi-beauty is steadily growing; therefore, the demand for Cosmetic RN's is on the rise.

Regimen

The Cosmetic RN supervises and delegates tasks to staff members. They work closely with patients, conduct treatment consultations, review client history and design treatment plans. A Cosmetic RN can perform non-surgical cosmetic treatments such as: laser hair removal, chemical peels, microdermabrasion, in some states Botox and cosmetic fillers.

Foundation

Current registered nurse license
College degree in nursing
Dermatology or medi- spa experience

Knowledge of cosmetic procedures and products
Excellent communication skills

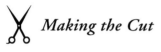 *Making the Cut*

An esthetic background or license is helpful, but not required. Experience received from working with a plastic surgeon's office, dermatologist or in a medical spa will excel your career.

 Highlights

This is an exceptional career opportunity for a nurse with training in cosmetic procedures.

@ *Tips*

Nurse.com

89. CRUISE SHIP HAIR STYLIST

The Make Up

Cruise ships are often referred to as cities floating on water. Cruise lines offer salon and spa services to both passengers and crew members, and provide a variety of hair care and body treatments.

Regimen

Stylists perform routine services such as: facials, waxing, cutting, styling, manicure and pedicure services. The stylists who perform these services are also considered specialized beauty therapists. Daily therapists consult clients, give service suggestions and recommend products to fit the customer's needs. It is important to implement the philosophy of the cruise line to ensure the client's experience is pleasing.

Foundation

Licensed cosmetologist
Service industry experience
Retail sales experience
Exceptional customer service skills

Must speak English, (bilingual a plus)
Desire to travel

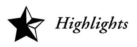 *Making the Cut*

Forward your professional resume and cover letter to a reputable staffing company that hires stylists for cruise ships. Beware of scams. There are companies that are frauds who do not actually hire people to work for cruise lines, but may appear legitimate. Contact the cruise line directly if you are suspicious about a company. Spend time studying other languages if you only speak English. This will help to make you more marketable and knowledgeable.

★ *Highlights*

Getting paid to do what you love while traveling to tourist attractions is worthwhile for those who love to be on the move. You'll learn about various cultures and meet people from all over the world.

@ *Tips*

Cruiselinejobs.com
Carnival.com

90. CRUISE SHIP MASSAGE THERAPIST

The Make Up

Like cruise ship hair specialists and stylists, massage therapists aboard cruise ships provide services for both crew members and passengers. Their primary goal is to achieve health and well being through their techniques and retail products.

Regimen

This therapy has evolved from not only using the hands but the forearms, elbows, products and natural elements to accomplish massage techniques. Sessions are scheduled based on the needs of the clients and can range from thirty to ninety minute sessions. Throughout the day, therapists work with clients to address circulatory, muscle, back and stress related issues.

Additional services provided by massage therapists are: weight reduction consulting, exercise program recommendations, water therapy variations, dry heat treatments, ultra violet light treatments and infrared light treatments.

 *Foundation*

Licensed massage therapist
Excellent listening skills
Great overall communication skills
Self starter
Member of a professional organization (a plus)
Bilingual (a plus)

 *Making the Cut*

Therapists must practice and take additional courses to master their techniques. Being professional, having a positive attitude, and exuding confidence will help you to secure the right job.

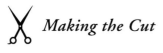 *Highlights*

Working on a cruise ship will allow you to develop as a professional and to gain cultural experience.

 Tips

Cruiselinejobs.com
Carnival.com

Amtamassage.org

91. HAIR SHOW COMPETITOR

The Make Up

Organisation Mondiale Coiffure (OMG) is the largest beauty organization in the word consisting of over sixty member countries and five hundred thousand salon owners. Teams are selected to represent the United States through the OMG American affiliate, the National Cosmetology Association (NCA). Competitions for teams and individuals are held periodically in different countries.

Regimen

Training is a top priority of hair show competitors. The competition requires participants to work a specified number of hours on mannequins to perfect their hair styles. In addition, continued enrollment in other national competitions is required during the off season. Competitors continue to have a rigorous schedule managing their full time salon or spa job and competition requirements.

 *Foundation*

Two or more years of professional experience
Current knowledge of trends, products and techniques
Creative style
Strong technical skills
NCA member
Continuing education classes

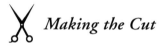 *Making the Cut*

One must be an active member of the National Cosmetology Association. Attend seminars, shows and actively participate in local, regional and national competitions. Make a name for yourself within the industry by sending your work into magazines and also participate in the North American Hairstyling Awards (NAHA). If you are a student, ask your school about the Junior Style Stars Competition or Skills USA to gain experience. Concentrate on your creativity, styles, shapes and colors. Be dedicated to growing as a stylist and a competitor.

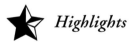 *Highlights*

Representing the United States is a privilege and honor. Competitors travel to various countries which host Hairworld. Doors will open for future career opportunities as you develop as a competitor.

@ *Tips*

Ncacares.org
Junior-style-stars.com
Skillsusa.org
Omchairworld.bauerundguse.de

92. HAIR TRANSPLANT TECH

The Make Up

This position requires one to assist the surgeon before, during, and after the medical procedure of a hair transplant. Technicians work in a medical environment and are responsible for preparing the surgery room prior to the medical procedure and cleaning the room after the procedure has taken place.

Regimen

This position requires one to chart medical records and to administer local anesthesia. In addition technicians help prepare and cut hair graphs. Other daily duties may include assisting the physician during surgical procedures.

 *Foundation*

High school diploma
Must have completed an accredited medical technician
or nursing program
One to two years technical assisting experience,
Must be a team player
Excellent communication skills
Excellent computer skills

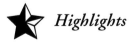 *Making the Cut*

Dependability is a key component to attaining this position.
Companies are looking for individuals who are serious about learning
and developing to become an excellent replacement specialist. Study
and spend time asking others who are currently in the position
questions prior to interviewing. You may even ask to shadow another
specialist for a day, just so you will have a clear understanding of
the position.

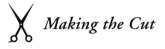 *Highlights*

Full benefits: health, dental, paid vacations, holidays and disability
insurance.

Tips

Hairtransplanttechnicians.com

93. IMAGE CONSULTANT

The Make Up

The stamp of approval from an image consultant has benefited a wide range of people and organizations. From recording artists to corporation executives, many choose to seek expert advise on etiquette, appearance, social skills, branding, customer service and more. One has options to work for a firm or independently.

Regimen

New and seasoned image consultants teach workshops and are considered experts in their field. Getting to know the client is the first step. Clients complete an analysis that asks questions about their occupation, lifestyle, personality, likes and dislikes. Corporations and other organizations also complete a front end analysis that reviews the company's structure and philosophy. Consultants study the industry specific to their clients and also study competitors of their clients in an effort to create the best strategies.

 *Foundation*

Fashion and marketing education
Degree in fashion and/or business (a plus)
Licensed cosmetologist a plus
Excellent communication skills
Negotiation skills
Excellent presentation skills
Certification (a plus), available through associations

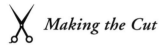 *Making the Cut*

You are a walking business card. Make sure that your image is professional and that you are an excellent representation of an image consultant. Volunteer to help youth, the unemployed, and others to learn and share your desire to make a difference.

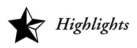 *Highlights*

Doing what you love will make your work days fun and joyful. Helping others achieve their goals is even more rewarding. This position can lead to writing books, freelance writing and producing training materials.

Tips

AICI.org

94. MORTUARY SERVICES

 *The Make Up*

Mortuary services include hair and make-up presentations of the deceased. Working in the funeral services industry as a full time, part time or contract employee provides career security. Professionals may consider working for multiple funeral homes or for one location. They are usually paid a flat fee per look.

Regimen

Many professionals are on call when employed in the mortuary service industry. Job duties include shampooing, cutting, coloring and styling hair. Make-up application is also a routine function and requires attention to detail. These beauty professionals work closely with funeral directors and family members to achieve a natural look.

Foundation

Diverse styling skills
Licensed cosmetologist
Sympathetic and caring personality
Strong work ethic
Flexible schedule

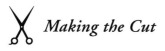

Making the Cut

Contact local funeral homes and ask to shadow to observe daily procedures as a first step. If you are comfortable and want to pursue a career in this field contact local funeral directors to obtain job opening lists.

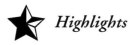

Highlights

This position offers a steady income for full time professionals and substantial supplemental income for part time and contract workers.

Tips

Craigslist.com

Funeralhomes.com

95. PERMANENT MAKE-UP SPECIALIST

The Make Up

This cosmetic technique produces results that resemble make-up applications to the face and body. It is used to correct problems as a result of disease, enhance features, and to camouflage scars. Permanent cosmetics, tattooing, micropigmentation and dermapigmentation are other names used for this procedure.

Regimen

Specialists give thorough consultations to learn the client's history, needs and wants prior to suggesting any type of procedure. Services include eyebrow forming and shaping, lip color, beauty marks, eyeliner and lash enhancements.

Foundation

Licensed esthetician or tattoo artist
Excellent communication skills
Current knowledge of permanent cosmetic procedures

Excellent customer service skills
Must take continuing education classes
Member of a professional esthetics or permanent make-up
association (a plus)

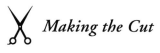 *Making the Cut*

Complete additional courses and certifications in permanent make-up application to improve your skills and credibility.

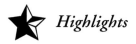 *Highlights*

Expand your current esthetics business or begin a new specialty as a permanent make-up specialist. Career opportunities are available in make-up and product development arenas.

 Tips

SPCP.org – Society of Permanent Cosmetic Professionals

96. PERSONAL SHOPPER

The Make Up

What a perfect fit for a stylist, make-up artist or freelance artist to add to their list of services. If you're like most beauty industry professionals then you love to shop. So just imagine how much fun it will be to shop and not have to use your own money. Personal shoppers purchase apparel, accessories, shoes and beauty products for clients. This position has similar attributes of an image consultant however personal shoppers do not focus on marketing, speaking and corporate image development. They are paid to shop for others and work for department stores, small shopping networks or independently.

Regimen

Give client consultations
Conduct a wardrobe and personality analysis
Provide suggestions based on the needs of the client
Work within the customer's budget
Meet deadlines set in the agreement

 *Foundation*

High school diploma
Dependable transportation
Excellent communication skills
Business management skills
Knowledge of fashion, beauty and technology
Friendly and honest

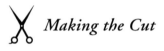 *Making the Cut*

You can attract clients through your personal style and professional presence. Brainstorm and use your professional talents to market your unique services. For example, some shoppers offer guided tours to groups which are tailored to their needs. Shoes, accessories, gifts and dresses are examples of areas where clients may need the special expertise of a personal shopper's guided tour.

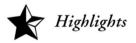 *Highlights*

Get paid to shop
Shop from home using the internet

@ *Tips*

Jobprofiles.monster.com
Entrepreneur.com
Fashionjunkie.com

97. RECRUITER

The Make Up

Promoting the company to clients is important, but it is just as important to promote career opportunities to potential receptionists, stylists and managers. Recruiters hire, interview, and search for future salon and spa employees. They have extensive knowledge of the beauty industry and the various opportunities available within the industry. This is usually a salaried position within a salon or spa organization. Recruiters work within a specific territory in close proximity to the location of the salon/spa(s).

Regimen

A daily routine may include conducting presentations and technical classes at beauty schools. Calling leads generated by shows, newspapers and online advertisements is also a key job responsibility. Attending job fairs and sponsoring salon events also helps recruiters to meet the high demand of staffing salons throughout their territory. Recruiters work hard to achieve goals set by management, but they also have great rewards.

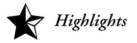 *Foundation*

Licensed cosmetologist
Three or more years of professional beauty industry experience
Current knowledge of technical skills and trends
Excellent presentation skills
Ability to build positive business relationships
Goal oriented
Salon management experience (a plus)

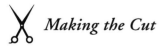 *Highlights*

Work from home
Networking
Travel
Ongoing training and development
Benefits

Making the Cut

Be an extraordinary communicator! Talking is a BIG part of this job, so it is of the utmost importance that recruiters speak well, with confidence and a professional demeanor. One must also be friendly, results oriented, and enjoy meeting and working with new people.

@ *Tips*

Haircuttery.com
Behindthechair.com

98. REFLEXOLOGIST

♀ *The Make Up*

Reflexology is the scientific art where one uses the hands, fingers and thumbs to apply pressure to reflex areas found in the feet, hands and outer ears. Derived from ancient healing techniques, this therapy treats insomnia, tension, circulatory, back, digestive and stress related problems. Reflexology also brings relief to many more conditions. The main goals are for reflexologists to improve gland, organ and body system functions.

① *Regimen*

Conduct a case history with each client
Perform an initial examination of the feet, hands, and outer ears

Apply treatment techniques to all areas of the feet
Schedule appointments
Make treatment and retail product recommendations

 *Foundation*

American Reflexology Certification Board Certificate (ARCB)
Completion of a reflexology training course
Excellent customer service skills
Marketing and networking skills
Current knowledge of therapy techniques

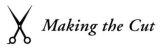 *Making the Cut*

Despite the differences between reflexology and massage therapy, some states have massage laws that may or may not exempt reflexologists. Most states do not have professional reflexology licensing requirements. Go to ARCB.net to review requirements and a list of reflexology training programs by state.

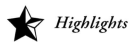 *Highlights*

One can establish a private practice with low start up costs. With educational workshops and certifications beauty industry professionals can add this service to their repertoire.

Tips

Acaret.org
Icr-reflexology.org
Arcb.net

99. STATE BOARD INSPECTOR

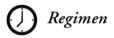 *The Make Up*

In order to provide consistent standards for health, safety, sanitation, licensure and other operational compliance guidelines, states regulate the operation of beauty industry organizations including salons, spas, barber shops, massage therapists, nail salons, and other independent beauty service providers. An inspector's role is designed to ensure beauty industry service organizations are in compliance with the rules, regulations and laws set by the state. Some inspector's positions are full time while many are considered part time contractual jobs.

Regimen

When one thinks of an inspector, you may imagine a salon or school getting word that an inspector is in the neighborhood, then running around frantically to make sure that every thing is in compliance. However, an inspector's job consists of much more. They prepare reports, investigate consumer complaints against licensed beauty industry professionals, gather information, offer testimony in hearings, and submit evidence to courts.

 *Foundation*

Must have experience in the practice of cosmetology (not required in all states)
Cosmetology instructor's license (not required in all states)
Experience analyzing data, gathering factual information and preparing reports
Valid driver's license and good driving record
Ability to build and maintain positive business relationships
Good communication skills
Most states will not allow one to be a salon owner or actively performing salon, spa or shop services

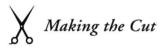 *Making the Cut*

Professionalism and additional characteristics like being well organized, timely, a good communicator, having excellent problem solving skills and paying attention to detail will help you to qualify for this position.

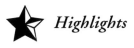 *Highlights*

This position can help prepare one to own a salon. If working part time one has the ability to work an additional job that is not a conflict of interest.

 Tips

Beautytech.com/st_boards.htm
Check your local state board of cosmetology for job opportunities. A list is provided in the back of the book.

100. TEMPORARY TATTOO ARTIST

The Make Up

There are two common methods that artists use to apply temporary tattoos, henna and airbrushing. Henna, a plant which produces a red-orange die has been used to dye hair, skin, nails and fabric for centuries. One of the most recent uses for this plant dye is temporary tattoos. Artists create designs using stencils or use free hand techniques. Designs can last up to five weeks. Airbrushing is the art of using an airbrush and ink to design temporary tattoos.

The designs last between three to five days and can be applied using various colors. Artists can work independently performing services for weddings, parties, trade shows and other events. Working for an event company is another option.

Regimen

Conduct consultations with clients
Schedule appointments and events
Build relationships with event planners
Review inventory
Order products and tools

Foundation

Licensed esthetician or cosmetologist (a plus)
Artistic
Business management and marketing skills
Assisting experience with an experienced temporary tattoo artist

Making the Cut

Master your presentation of creative and unique art designs. Work diligently to market yourself to individuals, businesses and groups.

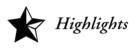 *Highlights*

Work as a full time independent contractor or add to the list of services you already perform as a licensed beauty industry professional.

@ *Tips*

Tribalinkproducts.com
Hennapage.com

101. TRICHOLOGIST

 The Make Up

Trichology is the scientific study of the hair and scalp. Although trichologists are not normally medical doctors, they do study the science of the hair and some medical doctors even study this division of science. The methods of trichology can be used in forensic studies and cases. Trichology jobs are generally part- time, independent positions.

Regimen

Conduct client consultations
Determine reason for hair loss
Diagnose possible scalp diseases and disorders
Recommend treatments and products
Schedule visits and follow up with clients
Research causes of hair loss

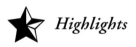

Foundation

High school diploma or GED
Excellent communication skills
Understanding of science
Diagnostic skills
Registered trichology association member

Highlights

This position is highly regarded in many countries. Helping to correct hair loss problems and scalp diseases is rewarding.

Tips

Hairscientists.org
Trichologists.org.uk

AFTERWORD

Daydreaming is a necessity for creative people. Sometimes I imagine myself vacationing on a beautiful beach and other times I'm being interviewed about the beauty industry on Good Morning America. Just like the young lady with the dream of having a salon on an airplane, my day dreaming may just pay off. For the next few moments think about what you absolutely love to do in the beauty industry. Don't make excuses by telling yourself "I can't do that because…". Excuses often keep us from pursuing and achieving our goals. Today instead of making excuses, make your mark.

"The trick to being successful is doing the things
that unsuccessful people will not do."

John Paul Dejoria

CAREER SEARCH ENGINES

Careerbuilder.com

Craigslist.com

Hotjobs.yahoo.com

Jobs.myspace.com

Monster.com

Opendoorjobs.com

Simplyhired.com

SALARY INFORMATION

Salary.com

SALON CHAINS

Cool Cuts 4 Kids – coolcuts4kids.com

Cost Cutters – costcutters.com

Fantastic Sams – fantasticsams.com

Great Clips – greatclips.com

Hair Cuttery – haircuttery.com

Hair Masters – hairmasterssalon.com

Pigtails and Crewcuts – pigtailsandcrewcuts.com

Regis – regissalons.com, regiscorp.com

Sassoon Salon – sassoon.com

Smart Style – smartstyle.com

Snipits – snipits.com

Sport Clips – sportclips.com

Supercuts – supercuts.com

Ulta – ulta.com

Toni & Guy – toniguy.com

PRODUCT COMPANIES

Andis – andis.com

American Crew- americancrew.com

Aveda – aveda.com

Avlon Industries, Inc. – avlon.com

Benefit Cosmetics – benefitcosmetics.com

Biosilk – biosilk.com

Bobbi Brown – bobbibrowncosmetics.com

Bonika Shears – bonikashears.com

Bronner Brothers – bronnerbros.com

Carol's Daughter – carolsdaughter.com

Chanel – chanel.com

Clairol – Clairol.com

Clinique – clinique.com

CND – Creative Nail Design – creativenaildesign.com

Dermalogica – dermalogica.com

Dudley- dudleyq.com

Essie Cosmetics – essie.com

Estee Lauder – esteelauder.com

Farouk – farouk.com

FHI Heat – fhiheat.com

GHD – ghdhair.com

Graham Webb – grahamwebb.com

Great Lengths – greatlengths.net

Hair U Wear – hairuwear.com

Helen of Troy – hotus.com

Joico – joico.com

Kenra – kenra.com

Kett Cosmetics – kettcosmetics.com

Lancome – lancome-usa.com

L'oreal – loreal.com

Mac – maccosmetics.com

Matrix – matrixbeautiful.com

McBride Research Laboratories- designessentials.com

Mizani – mizani-usa.com

Nars – narscosmetics.com

Nioxin – nioxin.com

OPI – opi.com

Oster – oster.com

Paul Mitchell – paulmitchell.com

Paul Brown – paulbrownhawaii.com

Pravanna – pravana.com

Redken 5th Avenue NYC – redken.com

Repechage – repechage.com

Revlon – Revlon.com

Rusk – rusk1.com

Sebastain – sebastianprofessional.com

Schwarzkopf - www.schwarzkopf.com

Scruples – scruples.com

Sexy Hair Concepts – sexyhair.com

TIGI – tigihaircare.com

TressAllure – tressallure.com

Tressa – tressa.com

Wella – wellusa.com

Your Name Professional Brand – yournamepro.com

SHOWS AND EVENTS

Americasbeautyshow.com

Bronnerbros.com/show

Cosmoprof.com

IBSnewyork.com

Iecsc.com - International Esthetics, Cosmetics & Spa Conference

Premiereshows.com

MAGAZINES

American Salon – americansalonmag.com

American Spa - americanspamag.com

Make Up Magazine – makeupmag.com

Modern Salon – modernsalon.com

Nail Pro – nailpro.com

Salon City – saloncity.com

Salon Today – salontoday.com

Spa Magazine – spamagazine.com

ASSOCIATIONS

American Association of Cosmetology Schools (AACS) –
beautyschools.org

American Electrology Association – electrology.com

Barbers International – barbersinternational.com

Cosmetology Advancement Foundation – cosmetology.org

International Guild of Professional Electrologists – igpe.org

National Accrediting Commission of Cosmetology Arts and
Sciences – naccas.org

National Beauty Culturist League – nbcl.org

National Cosmetology Association – ncacares.org

Reflexology Association – reflexology-usa.org

The American Massage Therapy Association – amtamassage.org

The Massage Therapy Foundation – massagetherapyfoundation.org

The Society for Clinical and Medical Hair Removal – scmhr.org

STATE BOARDS OF COSMETOLOGY, BARBERING AND ESTHETICS

Alabama – aboc.state.al.us

Alaska – dced.state.ak.us

Arkansas – Arkansas.gov/cos/

California - dca.ca.gov

Colorado - dora.state.co.us

Connecticut - ct.gov/dph/

Deleware - dpr.delaware.gov/boards/cosmetology

District of Columbia - dcra.washingtondc.gov

Florida – myflorida.com

Georgia - sos.georgia.gov/plb/cosmetology

Hawaii – ehawaii.gov

Idaho - ibol.idaho.gov/cos.htm

Illinois – idfpr.com

Indiana – in.gov

Iowa – idph.state.ia.us

Kansas - kansas.gov/kboc

Kentucky - kbhc.ky.gov

Louisiana - lsbc.louisiana.gov

Maine – maine.gov

Maryland - dllr.state.md.us

Massachusetts – mass.gov

Michigan – michigan.gov

Minnesota - bceboard.state.mn.us

Mississippi - msbc.state.ms.us

Missouri - pr.mo.gov/cosbar.asp

Montana – mt.gov

Nebraska - hhs.state.ne.us

Nevada - cosmetology.nv.gov

New Hampshire - nh.gov/cosmet

New Jersey - state.nj.us

New Mexico - rld.state.nm.us

New York - dos.state.ny.us

North Carolina - cosmetology.state.nc.us

Ohio - cos.ohio.gov

Oklahoma - state.ok.us

Oregon - oregon.gov

Pennsylvaina - dos.state.pa.us

Puerto Rico – estado.gobierno.pr

Rhode Island - health.state.ri.us

South Carolina - llr.state.sc.us

South Dakota - state.sd.us

Tennessee - tennessee.gov

Texas - license.state.tx.us

Utah - dopl.utah.gov

Vermont - vtprofessionals.org

Virginia - dpor.virginia.gov

Washington - dol.wa.gov/business/cosmetology

West Virginia - wvdhhr.org

Wisconsin - drl.wi.gov

Wyoming - cosmetology.state.wy.us

As an author and dynamic speaker, C. JEANINE FULTON empowers people to succeed. Currently, she is the Founder and Director of Operations for **Persona Market**, a training and publishing company targeting the beauty industry. *Industry In:Site*, a workbook magazine for future professionals is Persona Market's first publication, and *Industry In:Site, 101 Top Beauty Careers* is the company's second publication.

After completing her Bachelor of Science degree in Marketing in 1994, she pursued a career in the field of cosmetology. She also received a Master of Business Administration degree from **Nova Southeastern University** in 1999 while working both as a hair stylist and business professional. She was able to combine her marketing and cosmetic flair, and became a consultant for the world leading salon services company, **Regis Corporation**. She was also employed as a director at **Empire Beauty Schools**, America's largest provider of professional cosmetology education.